Global Capitalism
&
American Empire

GLOBAL CAPITALISM AND AMERICAN EMPIRE

Leo Panitch & Sam Gindin

Merlin Press
Fernwood Publishing

First published in 2004
by The Merlin Press Ltd.
PO Box 30705
London
WC2E 8QD
www.merlinpress.co.uk

This essay was first published in 2003 in
The New Imperial Challenge, Socialist Register 2004.

© Leo Panitch & Sam Gindin
The authors assert the right to be identified as the authors of this work

British Library Cataloguing in Publication Data is available from the
British Library

National Library of Canada Cataloguing in Publication Data
Panitch, Leo, 1945-
Global capitalism and American empire / Leo Panitch and Sam
Gindin.

Includes bibliographical references.
ISBN 1-55266-121-0

1. United States—Foreign economic relations.
2. United States—Foreign relations—1989-
3. Globalization. I. Gindin, Sam II. Title.
HF1455.P36 2003   337.73   C2003-905362-8

Published in the UK by The Merlin Press
ISBN 0850365422

Published in Canada by Fernwood Publishing
ISBN 1552661210

Printed in England by Antony Rowe Ltd, Chippenham

Acknowledgements

This essay, originally prepared for the *Socialist Register*'s 40th volume on 'The New Imperial Challenge', represents our initial attempt to formulate an new understanding of modern imperialism as part of our research project on 'Finance, Production and Empire: The Making of Global Capitalism'.

We wish to thank Adrian Howe and Tony Zurbrugg of Merlin Press for their initiative and skill in preparing the essay in this form, and also Greg Albo, Cenk Aygul, Patrick Bond, Dan Crow, Robert Cox, Bill Fletcher, Stephen Gill, Gerard Greenfield, Khashayar Khooshiyar, Martijn Konings, Colin Leys, Eric Newstadt, Chris Roberts, Donald Swartz and Alan Zuege for their earlier helpful comments and input.

Introduction

> 'American imperialism... has been made plausible
> and attractive in part by the insistence that it is not
> imperialistic.'
>
> Harold Innis, 1948[1]

The American empire is no longer concealed. In March 1999, the cover of the *New York Times Magazine* displayed a giant clenched fist painted in the stars and stripes of the US flag above the words: 'What The World Needs Now: For globalization to work, America can't be afraid to act like the almighty superpower that it is'. Thus was featured Thomas Friedman's 'Manifesto for a Fast World', which urged the United States to embrace its role as enforcer of the capitalist global order: '...the hidden hand of the market will never work without a hidden fist....The hidden fist that keeps the world safe for Silicon Valley's technologies is called the United States Army, Air Force, Navy and Marine Corps.' Four years later, in January 2003, when there was no longer any point in pretending the fist was hidden, the *Magazine* featured an essay by Michael Ignatieff

GLOBAL CAPITALISM AND AMERICAN EMPIRE

entitled 'The Burden': '…[W]hat word but "empire" describes the awesome thing that America is becoming? …Being an imperial power… means enforcing such order as there is in the world and doing so in the American interest.'[2] The words, 'The American Empire (Get Used To It)', took up the whole cover of the *Magazine*.

Of course, the American state's geopolitical strategists had already taken this tack. Among those closest to the Democratic Party wing of the state, Zbigniew Brzezinski did not mince words in his 1997 book, *The Grand Chessboard: American Primacy and Its Geostrategic Imperatives*, asserting that 'the three great imperatives of geo-political strategy are to prevent collusion and maintain security dependence amongst the vassals, to keep tributaries pliant, and to keep the barbarians from coming together.'[3] In the same year the Republican intellectuals who eventually would write the Bush White House's National Security Strategy founded the Project for a New American Century, with the goal of making imperial statecraft the explicit guiding principle of American policy.[4]

Most of what passes more generally for serious analysis in justifying the use of the term 'empire' in relation to the US today is really just an analogy, implicit or explicit, with imperial Rome. On the face of it, this is by no means absurd since, as an excellent recent book on the Roman Empire says, 'Romanization' could indeed be

> understood as the assimilation of the conquered nations to Roman culture and political worldview. The conquered became partners in running the

8

empire. It was a selective process that applied directly only to the upper level of subject societies but it trickled down to all classes with benefits for some, negative consequences for others.... Roman supremacy was based on a masterful combination of violence and psychological persuasion – the harshest punishment for those who challenged it, the perception that their power knew no limits and that rewards were given to those who conformed.[5]

But an analogy is not a theory. The neglect of any serious political economy or pattern of historical determination that would explain the emergence and reproduction of today's American empire, and the dimensions of structural oppression and exploitation pertaining to it, is striking. It serves as a poignant reminder of why it was Marxism that made the running in theorizing imperialism for most of the twentieth century. But as a leading Indian Marxist, Prabhat Patnaik, noted in his essay 'Whatever Happened to Imperialism?', by 1990 the topic had also 'virtually disappeared from the pages of Marxist journals' and even Marxists looked 'bemused' when the term was mentioned. The costs of this for the left were severe. The concept of imperialism has always been especially important as much for its emotive and mobilizing qualities as for its analytic ones. Indeed, in Patnaik's view, rather than 'a theoretically self-conscious silence', the 'very fact that imperialism has become so adept at "managing" potential challenges to its hegemony made us indifferent to its ubiquitous presence.'[6]

GLOBAL CAPITALISM AND AMERICAN EMPIRE

Yet the left's silence on imperialism also reflected severe analytic problems in the Marxist theory of imperialism. Indeed, this was obvious by the beginning of the 1970s – the last time the concept of imperialism had much currency – amidst complaints that the Marxist treatment of imperialism 'as an undifferentiated global product of a certain stage of capitalism' reflected its lack of 'any serious historical or sociological dimensions'.[7] As Giovanni Arrighi noted in 1978, 'by the end of the 60s, what had once been the *pride* of Marxism – the theory of imperialism – had become a tower of Babel, in which not even Marxists knew any longer how to find their way.'[8]

The confusion was apparent in debates in the early 1970s over the location of contemporary capitalism's contradictions. There were those who focused almost exclusively on the 'third world', and saw its resistance to imperialism as the sole source of transformation.[9] Others emphasized increasing contradictions within the developed capitalist world, fostering the impression that American 'hegemony' was in decline. This became the prevalent view, and by the mid-1980s the notion that 'the erosion of American economic, political, and military power is unmistakable' grew into a commonplace.[10] Although very few went back to that aspect of the Marxist theory of inter-imperial rivalry that suggested a military trial of strength, an era of intense regional economic rivalry was expected. As Glyn and Sutcliffe put it, all it was safe to predict was that without a hegemonic power 'the world economy will continue without a clear leader...'[11]

There was indeed no little irony in the fact that so many

continued to turn away from what they thought was the old-fashioned notion of imperialism, just when the ground was being laid for its renewed fashionability in the *New York Times*. Even after the 1990-91 Gulf War which, as Bruce Cumings pointed out, 'had the important goal of assuring American control of... Middle Eastern oil', you still needed 'an electron microscope to find "imperialism" used to describe the U.S. role in the world. ' The Gulf War, he noted, 'went forward under a virtual obliteration of critical discourse egged on by a complacent media in what can only be called an atmosphere of liberal totalism.'[12]

This continued through the 1990s, even while, as the recent book by the conservative Andrew Bacevich has amply documented, the Clinton Administration often outdid its Republican predecessors in unleashing military power to quell resistance to the continuing aggressive American pursuit of 'an open and integrated international order based on the principles of democratic capitalism.' Quoting Madeleine Albright, Clinton's Secretary of State, in 1998 ('If we have to use force, it is because we are America. We are the indispensable nation,') and, in 2000, Richard Haas, the State Department's Director of Policy Planning in the incoming Bush Administration, (calling on Americans finally to reconceive their state's 'global role from one of a traditional nation state to an imperial power'), Bacevich argues that the continuing avoidance of the term imperialism could not last. It was at best an 'astigmatism', and at worst 'an abiding preference for averting our eyes from the unflagging self-interest and large ambitions underlying all U.S. policy'.[13]

GLOBAL CAPITALISM AND AMERICAN EMPIRE

By the turn of the century, and most obviously once the authors of the Project for a New American Century were invested with power in Washington D.C., the term imperialism was finally back on even a good many liberals' lips. The popularity of Hardt and Negri's tome, *Empire*, had caught the new conjuncture even before the second war on Iraq. But their insistence (reflecting the widespread notion that the power of all nation states had withered in the era of globalization) that *'the United States does not, and indeed no nation state can today, form the center of an imperialist project'* was itself bizarrely out of sync with the times.[14]

The left needs a new theorization of imperialism, one that will transcend the limitations of the old Marxist 'stagist' theory of inter-imperial rivalry, and allow for a full appreciation of the historical factors that have led to the formation of a unique American informal empire. This will involve understanding how the American state developed the capacity to eventually incorporate its capitalist rivals, and oversee and police 'globalization' – i.e. the spread of capitalist social relations to every corner of the world. The theory must be able to answer the question of what made plausible the American state's insistence that it was not imperialistic, and how this was put into practice and institutionalized; and, conversely, what today makes implausible the American state's insistence that it is not imperialistic, and what effects its lack of concealment might have in terms of its attractiveness and its capacity to manage global capitalism and sustain its global empire.

Rethinking Imperialism

There is a structural logic to capitalism that tends to its expansion and internationalization. This was famously captured in Marx's description in the *Communist Manifesto* of a future that stunningly matches our present: 'The need of a constantly expanding market for its products chases the bourgeoisie over the whole surface of the globe. It must nestle everywhere, settle everywhere, establish connections everywhere... it creates a world after its own image.' But affirming Marx's prescience in this respect runs the risk of treating what is now called globalization as inevitable and irreversible. It must be remembered that Marx's words also seemed to apply at the end of the nineteenth century, when, as Karl Polanyi noted, '[o]nly a madman would have doubted that the international economic system was the axis of the material existence of the human race'.[15] Yet, as Polanyi was concerned to explain, far from continuing uninterrupted, there were already indications that the international economic system of the time was in the early stages of dissolution, and would soon collapse via two horrific world wars and the Great Depression.

GLOBAL CAPITALISM AND AMERICAN EMPIRE

The postwar reconstruction of the capitalist world order was a direct response on the part of the leading capitalist states to that earlier failure of globalization. Through the Bretton Woods infrastructure for a new liberal trading order the dynamic logic of capitalist globalization was once again unleashed. During the brief post-war 'golden age' – through the acceleration of trade, the new degree of direct foreign investment, and the growing internationalization of finance – capitalist globalization was revived, and was further invigorated through the neoliberal response to the economic crisis of the 1970s. The outcome of this crisis showed that the international effects of structural crises in accumulation are not predictable *a priori*. Of the three great structural crises of capitalism, the first (post-1870s) accelerated inter-imperialist rivalry and led to World War One and Communist revolution, while the second crisis (the Great Depression) actually reversed capitalism's internationalizing trajectory. Yet the crisis of the early 1970s was followed by a deepening, acceleration and extension of capitalist globalization. And while this promoted inter-regional economic competition, it did not produce anything like the old inter-imperial rivalry.

What this erratic trajectory from the nineteenth to the twenty-first century suggests is that the process of globalization is neither inevitable (as was conventionally assumed in the latter part of the nineteenth century and as is generally assumed again today), nor impossible to sustain (as Lenin and Polanyi, in their different ways, both contended). The point is that we need to distinguish between the

14

GLOBAL CAPITALISM AND AMERICAN EMPIRE

expansive tendency of capitalism and its actual history. A global capitalist order is always a contingent social construct: the actual development and continuity of such an order must be problematized. There is a tendency within certain strains of Marxism, as in much bourgeois analysis, to write theory in the present tense. We must not theorize history in such a way that the trajectory of capitalism is seen as a simple derivative of abstract economic laws. Rather, it is crucial to adhere to the Marxist methodological insight that insists, as Philip McMichael has argued, that it is necessary to '*historicize theory*, that is to problematize globalization as a relation immanent in capitalism, but with quite distinct material (social, political and environmental) relations across time and time-space... Globalization is not simply the unfolding of capitalist tendencies but a historically distinct project shaped, or complicated, by the contradictory relations of previous episodes of globalization.'[16]

Above all, the realization – or frustration – of capitalism's globalizing tendencies cannot be understood apart from the role played by the states that have historically constituted the capitalist world. The rise of capitalism is inconceivable without the role that European states played in establishing the legal and infrastructural frameworks for property, contract, currency, competition and wage-labour within their own borders, while also generating a process of uneven development (and the attendant construction of race) in the modern world. This had gone so far by the mid-to late nineteenth century that when capital expanded beyond the borders of a given European nation-state, it could do so

15

within new capitalist social orders that had been – or were just being – established by other states, or it expanded within a framework of formal or informal empire. Yet this was not enough to sustain capital's tendency to global expansion. No adequate means of overall global capitalist regulation existed, leaving the international economy and its patterns of accumulation fragmented, and thus fuelling the inter-imperial rivalry that led to World War I.

The classical theories of imperialism developed at the time, from Hobson's to Lenin's, were founded on a theorization of capitalist economic stages and crises. This was a fundamental mistake that has, ever since, continued to plague proper understanding.[17] The classical theories were defective in their historical reading of imperialism, in their treatment of the dynamics of capital accumulation, and in their elevation of a conjunctural moment of inter-imperial rivalry to an immutable law of capitalist globalization. A distinctive capitalist version of imperialism did not suddenly arrive with the so-called monopoly or finance-capital stage of capitalism in the late nineteenth century, as we argue below.

Moreover, the theory of crisis derived from the classical understanding of this period was mistakenly used to explain capitalism's expansionist tendencies. If capitalists looked to the export of capital as well as trade in foreign markets, it was not so much because centralization and concentration of capital had ushered in a new stage marked by the falling rate of profit, overaccumulation and/or underconsumption. Rather, akin to the process that had earlier led individual

GLOBAL CAPITALISM AND AMERICAN EMPIRE

units of capital to move out of their original location in a given village or town, it was the accelerated competitive pressures and opportunities, and the attendant strategies and emerging capacities of a developing capitalism, that pushed and facilitated the international expansionism of the late nineteenth and early twentieth centuries.

The classical theorists of imperialism also failed to apprehend adequately the spatial dimensions of this internationalization. They made too much of the export of goods and capital to what we now call the 'third world', because the latter's very underdevelopment limited its capacity to absorb such flows. And they failed to discern two key developments in the leading capitalist countries themselves. Rather than an exhaustion of consumption possibilities within the leading capitalist countries – a premise based on what Lenin's pamphlet *Imperialism* called 'the semi-starvation level of existence of the masses' – more and more Western working classes were then achieving increasing levels of private and public consumption.[18] And rather than the concentration of capital in these countries limiting the introduction of new products so that 'capital cannot find a field for profitable investment',[19] the very unevenness of on-going competition and technological development was introducing new prospects for internal accumulation. There was a deepening of capital at home, not just a spreading of capital abroad.

Far from being the highest stage of capitalism, what these theorists were observing was (as is now obvious) a relatively *early* phase of capitalism. This was so not just in terms of consumption patterns, financial flows and competition, but also in terms of the limited degree of foreign direct investment at the time, and the very rudimentary means that had then been developed for managing the contradictions associated with capitalism's internationalization.

It was, however, in their reductionist and instrumental treatment of the state that these theorists were especially defective.[20] Imperialism is not reducible to an economic explanation, even if economic forces are always a large part of it. We need, in this respect, to keep imperialism and capitalism as two distinct concepts. Competition amongst capitalists in the international arena, unequal exchange and uneven development are all aspects of capitalism itself, and their relationship to imperialism can only be understood through a theorization of the state. When states pave the way for their national capitals' expansion abroad, or even when they follow and manage that expansion, this can only be understood in terms of these states' relatively autonomous role in maintaining social order and securing the conditions of capital accumulation; and we must therefore factor state administrative capacities as well as class, cultural and military determinations into the explanation of the imperial aspect of this role.

Capitalist imperialism, then, needs to be understood through an extension of the theory of the capitalist state, rather than derived directly from the theory of economic stages or crises. And such a theory needs to comprise not only inter-imperial rivalry, and the conjunctural predominance of one imperial state, but also the structural penetration of former rivals by one imperial state. This means we need to historicize the theory, beginning by breaking with the conventional notion that the nature of modern imperialism was once and for all determined by the kinds of economic rivalries attending the stage of industrial concentration and financialization associated with turn-of-the-century 'monopoly capital'.

In fact, the transition to the modern form of imperialism may be located in the British state's articulation of its old mercantile formal empire with the informal empire it spawned in the mid-nineteenth century during the era of 'free trade'. Schumpeter's theory of imperialism as reflecting the atavistic role within capitalism of pre-capitalist exploiting and warrior classes, and both Kautsky's and Lenin's conception that mid-nineteenth century British industrial capital and its policy of free trade reflected a 'pure' capitalism antithetical or at least 'indifferent' to imperial expansion,[21] all derived from too crude an understanding of the separation of the economic from the political under capitalism. This lay at the root of the notion that the replacement of the era of free competition by the era of finance capital had ended that separation, leading to imperialist expansion, rivalry and war among the leading capitalist states.

Like contemporary discussions of globalization in the context of neoliberal 'free market' policies, the classical Marxist accounts of the nineteenth century era of free trade and its supersession by the era of inter-imperial rivalry also confusingly counterposed 'states' and 'markets'. In both cases there is a failure to appreciate the crucial role of the state in making 'free markets' possible and then to make them work. Just as the emergence of so-called 'laissez faire' under mid-nineteenth century industrial capitalism entailed a highly active state to effect the formal separation of the polity and economy, and to define and police the domestic social relations of a fully capitalist order, so did the external policy of free trade entail an extension of the imperial role along all of these dimensions on the part of the first state that 'created a form of imperialism driven by the logic of capitalism'.[22]

As Gallagher and Robinson showed 50 years ago, in a seminal essay entitled 'The Imperialism of Free Trade', the conventional notion (shared by Kautsky, Lenin and Schumpeter) that British free trade and imperialism did not mix was belied by innumerable occupations and annexations, the addition of new colonies, and especially by the importance of India to the Empire, between the 1840s and the 1870s. It was belied even more by the immense extension, for both economic and strategic reasons, of Britain's 'informal empire' via foreign investment, bilateral trade, 'friendship' treaties and gunboat diplomacy, so that 'mercantilist techniques of formal empire were being employed in the mid-Victorian age at the same time as informal techniques of free trade were being used in Latin America.

It is for this reason that attempts to make phases of imperialism correspond directly to phases in the economic growth of the metropolitan economy are likely to prove in vain…'[23] Gallagher and Robinson defined imperialism in terms of a *variable political function* 'of integrating new

GLOBAL CAPITALISM AND AMERICAN EMPIRE

regions into the expanding economy; its character is largely decided by the various and changing relationships between the political and economic elements of expansion in any particular region and time.'

> ...In other words, it is the politics as well as the economics of the informal empire which we have to include in the account...The type of political lien between the expanding economy and its formal and informal dependencies... has tended to vary with the economic value of the territory, the strength of its political structure, the readiness of its rulers to collaborate with British commercial and strategic purposes, the ability of the native society to undergo economic change without external control, the extent to which domestic and foreign political situations permitted British intervention, and, finally, how far European rivals allowed British policy a free hand.[24]

This is not to say there are not important differences between informal and formal empire. Informal empire requires the economic and cultural penetration of other states to be sustained by political and military coordination with other independent governments. The main factor that determined the shift to the extension of formal empires after the 1880s was not the inadequacy of Britain's relationship with its own informal empire, nor the emergence of the stage of monopoly or 'finance capital', but rather

21

GLOBAL CAPITALISM AND AMERICAN EMPIRE

Britain's inability to incorporate the newly emerging capitalist powers of Germany, the US and Japan into 'free trade imperialism'. Various factors determined this, including pre-capitalist social forces that did indeed remain important in some of these countries, nationalist sentiments that accompanied the development of capitalist nation-states, strategic responses to domestic class struggles as well as geopolitical and military rivalries, and especially the limited ability of the British state – reflecting also the growing separation between British financial and industrial capital – to prevent these other states trying to overturn the consequences of uneven development.

What ensued was the rush for colonies and the increasing organization of trade competition via protectionism (tariffs served as the main tax base of these states as well as protective devices for nascent industrial bourgeoisies and working classes). In this context, the international institutional apparatuses of diplomacy and alliances, British naval supremacy and the Gold Standard were too fragile even to guarantee equal treatment of foreign capital with national capital within each state (the key prerequisite of capitalist globalization), let alone to mediate the conflicts and manage the contradictions associated with the development of global capitalism by the late nineteenth century.

No less than Lenin, by 1914 Kautsky had accepted, following Hilferding's *Finance Capital*, that 'a brutal and violent' form of imperialist competition was 'a product of highly developed industrial capitalism.'[25] Kautsky was right

22

GLOBAL CAPITALISM AND AMERICAN EMPIRE

to perceive, however, that even if inter-imperial rivalry had led to war between the major capitalist powers, this was not an inevitable characteristic of capitalist globalization. What so incensed Lenin, with his proclivity for over-politicizing theory, was that Kautsky thought that all the major capitalist ruling classes, after 'having learned the lesson of the world war', might eventually come to revive capitalist globalization through a collaborative 'ultra-imperialism' in face of the increasing strength of an industrial proletariat that nevertheless still fell short of the capacity to effect a socialist transformation. But Kautsky himself made his case reductively, that is, by conceiving his notion of ultra-imperialism from, as he repeatedly put it, 'a purely economic standpoint', rather than in terms of any serious theory of the state.

Moreover, had Kautsky put greater stress on his earlier perception (in 1911) that 'the United States is the country that shows us our social future in capitalism', and discerned the capacity of the newly emerging informal American empire for eventually penetrating and coordinating the other leading capitalist states, rather than anticipating an equal alliance amongst them, he might have been closer to the mark in terms of what finally actually happened after 1945. But what could hardly yet be clearly foreseen were the developments, both inside the American social formation and state as well as internationally, that allowed American policy makers to think that 'only the US had the power to grab hold of history and make it conform.'[26]

23

The American Republic: 'Extensive Empire and Self-Government'

The central place the United States now occupies within global capitalism rests on a particular convergence of structure and history. In the abstract, we can identify specific institutions as reflecting the structural power of capitalism. But what blocks such institutions from emerging and what, if anything, opens the door to their development, is a matter of historical conjunctures. The crucial phase in the reconstruction of global capitalism – after the earlier breakdowns and before the reconstitution of the last quarter of the twentieth century – occurred during and after World War II. It was only after (and as a state-learned response to) the disasters of Depression and the Second World War that capitalist globalization obtained a new life. This depended, however, on the emergence and uneven historical evolution of a set of structures developed under the leadership of a unique *agent*: the American imperial state.

The role the United States came to play in world

GLOBAL CAPITALISM AND AMERICAN EMPIRE

capitalism was not inevitable but nor was it merely accidental: it was not a matter of teleology but of capitalist history. The capacity it developed to 'conjugate' its '*particular* power with the *general* task of coordination' in a manner that reflected 'the particular matrix of its own social history', as Perry Anderson has recently put it, was founded on 'the attractive power of US models of production and culture... increasingly unified in the sphere of consumption.' Coming together here were, on the one hand, the invention in the US of the modern corporate form, 'scientific management' of the labour process, and assembly-line mass production; and, on the other, Hollywood-style 'narrative and visual schemas stripped to their most abstract', appealing to and aggregating waves of immigrants through the 'dramatic simplification and repetition'.[27] The dynamism of American capitalism and its worldwide appeal combined with the universalistic language of American liberal democratic ideology to underpin a capacity for informal empire far beyond that of nineteenth century Britain's. Moreover, by spawning the modern multinational corporation, with foreign direct investment in production and services, the American informal empire was to prove much more penetrative of other social formations.

Yet it was not only the economic and cultural formation of American capitalism, but also the formation of the American state that facilitated a new informal empire. Against Anderson's impression that the American state's constitutional structures lack the 'carrying power' of its economic and cultural ones (by virtue of being 'moored to

GLOBAL CAPITALISM AND AMERICAN EMPIRE

eighteenth century arrangements')[28] stands Thomas Jefferson's observation in 1809 that 'no constitution was ever before as well-calculated for extensive empire and self-government.'[29] Hardt and Negri were right to trace the pre-figuration of what they call 'Empire' today back to the American constitution's incorporation of Madisonian 'network power'.[30] This entailed not only checks and balances within the state apparatus, but the notion that the greater plurality of interests incorporated within an extensive and expansive state would guarantee that the masses would have no common motive or capacity to come together to check the ruling class.[31] Yet far from anticipating the sort of decentred and amorphous power that Hardt and Negri imagine characterized the US historically (and characterizes 'Empire' today), the constitutional framework of the new American state gave great powers to the central government to expand trade and make war. As early as 1783, what George Washington already spoke of ambitiously as 'a rising empire'[32] was captured in the Federalist Paper XI image of 'one great American system superior to the control of all transatlantic force or influence and able to dictate the terms of connection between the old and the new world!'[33]

The notion of empire employed here was conceived, of course, in relation to the other mercantile empires of the eighteenth century. But the state which emerged out of the ambitions of the 'expansionist colonial elite',[34] with Northern merchants (supported by artisans and commercial farmers) and the Southern plantation-owners allying against Britain's formal mercantile empire, evinced from its begin-

26

GLOBAL CAPITALISM AND AMERICAN EMPIRE

nings a trajectory leading to capitalist development and informal empire. The initial form this took was through territorial expansion westward, largely through the extermination of the native population, and blatant exploitation not only of the black slave population but also debt-ridden subsistence farmers and, from at least the 1820s on, an emerging industrial working class. Yet the new American state could still conceive of itself as embodying republican liberty, and be widely admired for it, largely due to the link between 'extensive empire and self-government' embedded in the federal constitution. In Bernard DeVoto's words, 'The American empire would not be mercantilist but in still another respect something new under the sun: the West was not to be colonies but states.'[35]

And the 'state rights' of these states were no mirage: they reflected the two different types of social relations – slave and free – that composed each successive wave of new states and by 1830 limited the activist economic role of the federal state. After the domestic inter-state struggles that eventually led to civil war, the defeat of the plantocracy and the dissolution of slavery, the federal constitution provided a framework for the unfettered domination of an industrial capitalism with the largest domestic market in the world, obviating any temptation towards formal imperialism via territorial conquest abroad.[36] The outcome of the Civil War allowed for a reconstruction of the relationship between financial and industrial capital and the federal state, inclining state administrative capacities and policies away from mercantilism and towards extended capitalist reproduc-

GLOBAL CAPITALISM AND AMERICAN EMPIRE

tion.[37] Herein lies the significance that Anderson himself attaches to the evolving juridical form of the American state, whereby 'unencumbered property rights, untrammeled litigation, the invention of the corporation' led to

> what Polanyi most feared, a juridical system disembedding the market as far as possible from ties of custom, tradition or solidarity, whose very abstraction from them later proved – American firms like American films – exportable and reproducible across the world, in a way that no other competitor could quite match. The steady transformation of international merchant law and arbitration in conformity with US standards is witness to the process.[38]

The expansionist tendencies of American capitalism in the latter half of the nineteenth century (reflecting pressures from domestic commercial farmers as much as from the industrialists and financiers of the post-civil war era) were even more apt to take informal forms than had those of British capitalism, even though they were not based on a policy of free trade. The modalities were initially similar, and they began long before the Spanish-American War of 1898, which is usually seen as the start of US imperial expansion. This was amply documented in a paper boldly called 'An Indicator of Informal Empire' prepared for the US Center for Naval Analysis: between 1869 and 1897 the US Navy made no less than 5,980 ports of call to protect American

28

GLOBAL CAPITALISM AND AMERICAN EMPIRE

commercial shipping in Argentina, Brazil Chile, Nicaragua, Panama, Columbia and elsewhere in Latin America.[39] Yet the establishment of colonies in Puerto Rico and the Philippines and the annexation of Hawaii 'was a deviation … from the typical economic, political and ideological forms of domination already characteristic of American imperialism.'[40] Rather, it was through American foreign direct investment and the modern corporate form – epitomized by the Singer Company establishing itself as the first multinational corporation when it jumped the Canadian tariff barrier to establish a subsidiary to produce sewing machines for prosperous Ontario wheat farmers – that the American informal empire soon took shape in a manner quite distinct from the British one.[41]

The articulation of the new informal American empire with military intervention was expressed by Theodore Roosevelt in 1904 in terms of the exercise of 'international police power', in the absence of other means of international control, to the end of establishing regimes that know 'how to act with reasonable efficiency and decency in social and political matters' and to ensure that each such regime 'keeps order and pays its obligations': '[A] nation desirous both of securing respect for itself and of doing good to others [Teddy Roosevelt declared, in language that has now been made very familiar again] must have a force adequate for the work which it feels is allotted to it as its part of the general world duty… A great free people owes to itself and to all mankind not to sink into helplessness before the powers of evil.'[42]

GLOBAL CAPITALISM AND AMERICAN EMPIRE

The American genius for presenting its informal empire in terms of the framework of universal rights reached its apogee under Woodrow Wilson. It also reached the apogee of hypocrisy, especially at the Paris Peace Conference, where Keynes concluded Wilson was 'the greatest fraud on earth'.[43] Indeed, it was not only the US Congress's isolationist tendencies, but the incapacity of the American presidential, treasury and military apparatuses, that explained the failure of the United States to take responsibility for leading European reconstruction after World War One. The administrative and regulatory expansion of the American state under the impact of corporate liberalism in the Progressive era,[44] and the spread of American direct investment through the 1920s (highlighted by General Motor's purchase of Opel immediately before the Great Depression, completing the 'virtual division' of the German auto industry between GM and Ford)[45] were significant developments. Yet it was only during the New Deal that the US state really began to develop the modern planning capacities that would, once they were redeployed in World War II, transform and vastly extend America's informal imperialism.[46]

Amidst the remarkable depression-era class struggles these capacities were limited by 'political fragmentation, expressed especially in executive-congressional conflict, combined with deepening tensions between business and government...'[47] America's entry into World War II, however, not only resolved 'the statebuilding impasse of the late 1930s' but also provided 'the essential underpinnings for

30

GLOBAL CAPITALISM AND AMERICAN EMPIRE

postwar U.S. governance.' As Brian Waddell notes in his outstanding study of the transition from the state-building of the Depression to that of World War II:

> The requirements of total war... revived corporate political leverage, allowing corporate executives inside and outside the state extensive influence over wartime mobilization policies... Assertive corporate executives and military officials formed a very effective wartime alliance that not only blocked any augmentation of the New Dealer authority but also organized a powerful alternative to the New Deal. International activism displaced and supplanted New Deal domestic activism.

Thus was the stage finally set for a vastly extended and much more powerful informal US empire outside its own hemisphere.

The American Reconstruction of a Capitalist World Order

The shift of U.S. state capacities towards realizing internationally-interventionist goals versus domestically-interventionist ones'[48] was crucial to the revival of capitalism's globalizing tendencies after World War II. This not only took place through the wartime reconstruction of the American state, but also through the more radical postwar reconstruction of all the states at the core of the old inter-imperial rivalry. And it also took place alongside – indeed it led to – the multiplication of new states out of the old colonial empires. Among the various dimensions of this new relationship between capitalism and imperialism, the most important was that *the densest imperial networks and institutional linkages, which had earlier run north-south between imperial states and their formal or informal colonies, now came to run between the US and the other major capitalist states.*

What Britain's informal empire had been unable to manage (indeed hardly to even contemplate) in the nine-

GLOBAL CAPITALISM AND AMERICAN EMPIRE

teenth century was now accomplished by the American informal empire, which succeeded in integrating all the other capitalist powers into an effective system of coordination under its aegis. Even apart from the U.S. military occupations, the devastation of the European and Japanese economies and the weak political legitimacy of their ruling classes at the war's end created an unprecedented opportunity which the American state was now ready and willing to exploit. In these conditions, moreover, the expansion of the informal American empire after World War II was hardly a one-way (let alone solely coercive) imposition – it was often 'imperialism by invitation'.[49]

However important was the development of the national security state apparatus and the geostrategic planning that framed the division of the world with the USSR at Yalta,[50] no less important was the close attention the Treasury and State Department paid during the war to plans for relaunching a coordinated liberal trading regime and a rule-based financial order. This was accomplished by manipulating the debtor status of the US's main allies, assisted by the complete domination of the dollar as a world currency and the fact that 50% of world production was now accounted for by the U.S. economy. The American state had learned well the lesson of its post-World War I incapacity to combine liberal internationalist rhetoric with an institutional commitment to manage an international capitalist order.

Through the very intricate joint planning of the British and American Treasuries during the war[51] – i.e. through the

33

GLOBAL CAPITALISM AND AMERICAN EMPIRE

process that led to Bretton Woods – the Americans not only ensured that the British were 'accepting some obligation to modify their domestic policy in light of its international effects on stability', but also ensured the liquidation of the British Empire by 'throwing Britain into the arms of America as a supplicant, and therefore subordinate; a subordination masked by the illusion of a "special relationship" which continues to this day'.[52]

But it was by no means only the US dollars that were decisive here, nor was Britain the only object of America's new informal empire. A pamphlet inserted in *Fortune* magazine in May 1942 on 'The U.S. in a New World: Relations with Britain' set out a program for the 'integration of the American and British economic systems as the foundation for a wider postwar integration':

> … if a world order is to arise out of this war, it is realistic to believe that it will not spring full-blown from a conference of fifty states held at given date to draw up a World Constitution. It is more likely to be the gradual outgrowth of the wartime procedures now being developed… If the U.S. rejects a lone-wolf imperialism and faces the fact that a League of Nations or some other universal parliament cannot be set up in the near future…[this] does not prevent America from approaching Britain with a proposal for economic integration as a first step towards a general reconstruction procedure. Unless we can reach a

34

meeting of minds with Britain and the Dominions on these questions it is utopian to expect wider agreement among all the United Nations.[53]

This pamphlet was accompanied by a lengthy collective statement[54] by the editors of *Fortune* and *Time* and *Life* magazines which began with the premise that 'America will emerge as the strongest single power in the postwar world, and...it is therefore up to it to decide what kind of postwar world it wants.' They called, in this context, for 'mutual trust between the businessman and his government' after the tensions of the New Deal, so that government could exercise its responsibilities both 'to use its fiscal policy as a balance wheel, and to use its legislative and administrative power to promote and foster private enterprise, by removing barriers to its natural expansion...' This would produce 'an expansionist context in which tariffs, subsidies, monopolies, restrictive labor rules, plantation feudalism, poll taxes, technological backwardness, obsolete tax laws, and all other barriers to further expansion can be removed.'

While recognizing that 'the uprising of [the] international proletariat... the most significant fact of the last twenty years... means that complete international free trade, as Cobden used to preach it and Britain used to practice it, is no longer an immediate political possibility', nevertheless free trade between the US and the Britain would be 'a jolt both economies need' and on this basis 'the area of freedom would spread – gradually through the British Dominions, through Latin America, perhaps

35

GLOBAL CAPITALISM AND AMERICAN EMPIRE

someday through the world. For universal free trade, not bristling nationalism, is the *ultimate* goal of a rational world.' And in terms that were uncharacteristically direct, the editors called this a new imperialism:

> Thus, a new American 'imperialism', if it is to be called that, will – or rather can – be quite different from the British type. It can also be different from the premature American type that followed our expansion in the Spanish war. American imperialism can afford to complete the work the British started; instead of salesmen and planters, its representatives can be brains and bulldozers, technicians and machine tools. American imperialism does not need extra-territoriality; it can get along better in Asia if the tuans and sahibs stay home… Nor is the U.S. afraid to help build up industrial rivals to its own power… because we know industrialization stimulates rather than limits international trade… This American imperialism sounds very abstemious and high-minded. It is nevertheless a feasible policy for America, because friendship, not food, is what we need most from the rest of the world.

The immense managerial capacity the American state had developed to make this perspective a reality was nowhere more clearly confirmed than at the Bretton Woods conference in 1944. The Commission responsible for establishing the IMF was chaired and tightly controlled

36

GLOBAL CAPITALISM AND AMERICAN EMPIRE

by the 'New Dealer' Harry Dexter White for the American Treasury, and even though Keynes chaired the Commission responsible for planning what eventually became the World Bank, and though the various committees under him were also chaired by non-Americans, 'they had American rapporteurs and secretaries, appointed and briefed by White', who also arranged for 'a conference journal to be produced every day to keep everyone informed of the main decisions. At his disposal were 'the mass of stenographers working day and night [and] the boy scouts acting as pages and distributors of papers' — all written in a 'legal language which made everything difficult to understand [amidst] the great variety of unintelligible tongues'. This was the 'controlled Bedlam' the American Treasury wanted in order to 'make easier the imposition of a *fait accompli*.'

It was in this context that every delegation finally decided 'it was better to run with the US Treasury than its disgruntled critics, "who [Keynes put it] do not know their own mind and have no power whatever to implement their promises."' The conference ended with Keynes's tribute to a process in which 44 countries 'had been learning to work together so that "the brotherhood of man will become more than a phrase." The delegates applauded wildly. "The Star Spangled Banner" was played'.[55]

With the IMF and World Bank headquarters established at American insistence in Washington, D.C., a pattern was set for international economic management among all the leading capitalist countries that continues to this day, one in which even when European or Japanese finance ministries

GLOBAL CAPITALISM AND AMERICAN EMPIRE

and central banks propose, the US Treasury and Federal Reserve dispose.[56] The dense institutional linkages binding these states to the American empire were also institutionalized, of course, through the institutions of NATO, not to mention the hub-and-spokes networks binding each of the other leading capitalist states to the intelligence and security apparatuses of the US as part of the strategy of containment of Communism during the Cold War. These interacted with economic networks, as well as with new propaganda, intellectual and media networks, to explain, justify and promote the new imperial reality.

Most of those who stress the American state's military and intelligence links with the coercive apparatuses of Europe and Japan tend to see the roots of this in the dynamics of the Cold War.[57] Yet as Bacevich, looking at American policy from the perspective of the collapse of the USSR, has recently said:

> To conceive of US grand strategy from the late 1940's through the 1980's as 'containment' – with no purpose apart from resisting the spread of Soviet power – is not wrong, but it is incomplete…[S]uch a cramped conception of Cold War strategy actively impedes our understanding of current US policy…No strategy worthy of the name is exclusively passive or defensive in orientation…US grand strategy during the Cold War required not only containing communism but also taking active measures to

38

GLOBAL CAPITALISM AND AMERICAN EMPIRE

open up the world politically, culturally, and, above all, economically – which is precisely what policymakers said they intended to do.[58]

What an exclusive concentration on the foreign policy, intelligence and coercive apparatuses also obscures is how far the American 'Protectorate System' (as Peter Gowan calls it), was part of actually 'alter[ing] the character of the capitalist core.' For it entailed the 'internal transformation of social relations within the protectorates in the direction of the American "Fordist" system of accumulation [that] opened up the possibility of a vast extension of their *internal markets*, with the working class not only as source of expanded surplus value but also an increasingly important consumption centre for *realizing* surplus value.'[59] While the new informal empire still provided room for the other core states to act as 'autonomous organizing centres of capital accumulation', the emulation of US technological and managerial 'Fordist' forms (initially organized and channelled through the post-war joint 'productivity councils') was massively reinforced by American foreign direct investment.

Here too, the core of the American imperial network shifted towards to the advanced capitalist countries, so that between 1950 and 1970 Latin America's share of total American FDI fell from 40 to under 20 percent, while Western Europe's more than doubled to match the Canadian share of over 30 percent.[60] It was hardly surprising that acute outside observers such as Raymond Aron and Nicos Poulantzas saw in Europe a tendential

39

'Canadianization' as the model form of integration into the American empire.[61]

None of this meant, of course, that the north-south dimension of imperialism became unimportant. But it did mean that the other core capitalist countries' relationships with the third world, including their ex-colonies, were imbricated with American informal imperial rule. The core capitalist countries might continue to benefit from the north-south divide, but any interventions had to be either American-initiated or at least have American approval (as Suez proved). Only the American state could arrogate to itself the right to intervene against the sovereignty of other states (which it repeatedly did around the world) and only the American state reserved for itself the 'sovereign' right to reject international rules and norms when necessary. It is in this sense that only the American state was actively 'imperialist'.

Though informal imperial rule seemed to place the 'third world' and the core capitalist countries on the same political and economic footing, both the legacy of the old imperialism and the vast imbalance in resources between the Marshall Plan and third world development aid reproduced global inequalities. The space was afforded the European states to develop internal economic coherence and growing domestic markets in the post-war era, and European economic integration was also explicitly encouraged by the US precisely as a mechanism for the 'European rescue of the nation-state', in Alan Milward's apt formulation.[62] But this contrasted with American dislike of

40

import-substitution industrialization strategies adopted by states in the south, not to mention US hostility to planned approaches to developing the kind of auto-centric economic base that the advanced capitalist states had created for themselves before they embraced a liberal international economic order. (Unlike the kind of geostrategic concerns that predominated in the American wars in Korea and Vietnam, it was opposition to economic nationalism that determined the US state's involvement in the overthrow of numerous governments from Iran to Chile.). The predictable result – given limits on most of the third world's internal markets, and the implications of all the third world states competing to break into international markets – was that global inequalities increased, even though a few third world states, such as South Korea, were able to use the geostrategic space that the new empire afforded them to develop rapidly and narrow the gap.

Still, in general terms, the new informal form of imperial rule, not only in the advanced capitalist world but also in those regions of the third world where it held sway, was characterized by the penetration of borders, not their dissolution. It was not through formal empire, but rather through the reconstitution of states as integral elements of an informal American empire, that the international capitalist order was now organized and regulated. Nation states remained the primary vehicles through which (a) the social relations and institutions of class, property, currency, contract and markets were established and reproduced; and (b) the international accumulation of capital was carried out. The vast expansion of direct foreign investment worldwide, whatever the shifting regional shares of the total, meant that far from capital escaping the state, it expanded its dependence on *many* states. At the same time, capital as an effective social force within any given state now tended to include both foreign capital and domestic capital with international linkages and ambitions. Their interpenetration made the notion of distinct national bourgeoisies – let alone rivalries between them in any sense analogous to those that led to World War I – increasingly anachronistic.

A further dimension of the new relationship between capitalism and empire was thus the *internationalization of the state*, understood as a state's acceptance of responsibility for managing its domestic capitalist order in way that contributes to managing the international capitalist order.[63] For the American imperial state, however, the internationalization of the state had a special quality. It entailed defining the American national interest in terms of acting not only on behalf of its own capitalist class but also on behalf of the extension and reproduction of global capitalism. The determination of what this required continued to reflect the particularity of the American state and social formation, but it was increasingly inflected towards a conception of the American state's role as that of ensuring the survival of 'free enterprise' in the US itself through its promotion of free enterprise and free trade internationally. This was classically articulated in President Truman's famous speech against isolationism at Baylor University in March 1947:

GLOBAL CAPITALISM AND AMERICAN EMPIRE

Now, as in the year 1920, we have reached a turning point in history. National economies have been disrupted by the war. The future is uncertain everywhere. Economic policies are in a state of flux. In this atmosphere of doubt and hesitation, the decisive factor will be the type of leadership that the United States gives the world. We are the giant of the economic world. Whether we like it or not, the future pattern of economic relations depends upon us... Our foreign relations, political and economic, are indivisible.[64]

The internationalization of the Americans state was fully encapsulated in National Security Council document NSC-68 of 1950, which (although it remained 'Top Secret' until 1975) Kolko calls 'the most important of all postwar policy documents'. It articulated most clearly the goal of constructing a 'world environment in which the American system can survive and flourish... Even if there were no Soviet Union we would face the great problem... [that] the absence of order among nations is becoming less and less tolerable.'[65]

43

The Reconstitution of American Empire in the Neoliberal Era

This pattern of imperial rule was established in the post-war period of reconstruction, a period that, for all of the economic dynamism of 'the golden age', was inherently transitional. The very notion of 'reconstruction' posed the question of what might follow once the European and Japanese economies were rebuilt and became competitive with the American, and once the benign circumstances of the post-war years were exhausted.[66] Moreover, peasants' and workers' struggles and rising economic nationalism in the third world, and growing working class militancy in the core capitalist countries, were bound to have an impact both on capital's profits and on the institutions of the post-war institutional order.

In less than a generation, the contradictions inherent in the Bretton Woods agreement were exposed. By the time European currencies became fully convertible in 1958, almost all the premises of the 1944 agreement were already

GLOBAL CAPITALISM AND AMERICAN EMPIRE

in question. The fixed exchange rates established by that agreement depended on the capital controls that most countries other than the US maintained after the war.[67] Yet the very internationalization of trade and direct foreign investment that Bretton Woods promoted (along with domestic innovations and competition in mortgages, credit, investment banking and brokerage that strengthened the capacity of the financial sector within the United States) contributed to the restoration of a global financial market, the corresponding erosion of capital controls, and the vulnerability of fixed exchange rates.[68]

Serious concerns over a return to the international economic fragmentation and collapse of the interwar period were voiced by the early sixties as the American economy went from creditor to debtor status, the dollar moved from a currency in desperately short supply to one in surplus, and the dollar–gold standard, which had been embedded in Bretton Woods, began to crumble.[69] But in spite of new tensions between the US and Europe and Japan, the past was not replayed. American dominance, never fundamentally challenged, would come to be reorganized on a new basis, and international integration was not rolled back but intensified.

This reconstitution of the global order, like earlier developments within global capitalism, was not inevitable. What made it possible – what provided the American state the time and political space to renew its global ambitions – was that by the time of the crisis of the early seventies American ideological and material penetration of, and integration

45

GLOBAL CAPITALISM AND AMERICAN EMPIRE

with, Europe and Japan was sufficiently strong to rule out any retreat from the international economy or any fundamental challenge to the leadership of the American state.

The United States had, of course, established itself as the military protectorate of Europe and Japan, and this was maintained while both were increasingly making their way into American markets. But the crucial factor in cementing the new imperial bond was foreign direct investment as the main form now taken by capital export and international integration in the post-war period. American corporations, in particular, were evolving into the hubs of increasingly dense host-country and cross-border networks amongst suppliers, financiers, and final markets (thereby further enhancing the liberalized trading order as a means of securing even tighter international networks of production). Even where the initial response to the growth of such American investment was hostile, this generally gave way to competition to attract that investment, and then emulation to meet 'the American challenge' through counter-investments in the United States.

Unlike trade, American FDI directly affected the class structures and state formations of the other core countries.[70] Tensions and alliances that emerged within domestic capitalist classes could no longer be understood in purely 'national' terms. German auto companies, for example, followed American auto companies in wanting European-wide markets; and they shared mutual concerns with the American companies inside Germany, such as over the cost of European steel. They had reason to be wary of policies that discriminated in favour of European companies but

46

GLOBAL CAPITALISM AND AMERICAN EMPIRE

might, as a consequence, compromise the treatment of their own growing interest in markets and investments in the United States. And if instability in Latin America or other 'trouble spots' threatened their own international investments, they looked primarily to the US rather than their own states to defend them.

With American capital a social force within each European country, domestic capital tended to be 'dis-articulated' and no longer represented by a coherent and independent national bourgeoisie.[71] The likelihood that domestic capital might challenge American dominance – as opposed to merely seeking to renegotiate the terms of American leadership – was considerably diminished. Although the West European and Japanese economies had been rebuilt in the post-war period, the nature of their integration into the global economy tended to tie the successful reproduction of their own social formations to the rules and structures of the American-led global order. However much the European and Japanese states may have wanted to renegotiate the arrangements struck in 1945, now that only 25% of world production was located in the U.S. proper, neither they nor their bourgeoisies were remotely interested in challenging the hegemony that the American informal empire had established over them. 'The question for them', as Poulantzas put it in the early seventies, 'is rather to reorganize a hegemony that they still accept...; what the battle is actually over is the share of the cake.'[72]

It was in this context that the internationalization of the state became particularly important. In the course of the protracted and often confused renegotiations in the 1970s

47

Global Capitalism and American Empire

of the terms that had, since the end of World War II, bound Europe and Japan to the American empire, all the nation states involved came to accept a responsibility for creating the necessary *internal* conditions for sustained *international* accumulation, such as stable prices, constraints on labour militancy, national treatment of foreign investment and no restrictions on capital outflows. The real tendencies that emerged out of the crisis of the 1970s were (to quote Poulantzas again) 'the internalized transformations of the national state itself, aimed at taking charge of the internationalization of public functions on capital's behalf.'[73] Nation states were thus not fading away, but adding to their responsibilities.

Not that they saw clearly what exactly needed to be done. The established structures of the post–1945 order did not, in themselves, provide a resolution to the generalized pressures on profit rates in the United States and Europe. They did not suggest how the U.S. might revive its economic base so as to consolidate its rule. Nor did they provide an answer to how tensions and instabilities would be managed in a world in which the American state was not omnipotent but rather depended, for its rule, on working through other states. The contingent nature of the new order was evidenced by the fact that a 'solution' only emerged at the end of the seventies, two full decades after the first signs of trouble, almost a decade after the dollar crisis of the early seventies, and after a sustained period of false starts, confusions, and uncertain experimentation.[74]

The first and most crucial response of the Nixon administration, the dramatic end to the convertibility of the

48

GLOBAL CAPITALISM AND AMERICAN EMPIRE

American dollar in 1971, restored the American state's economic autonomy in the face of a threatened rush to gold; and the subsequent devaluation of the American dollar did, at least temporarily, correct the American balance of trade deficit. Yet that response hardly qualified as a solution to the larger issues involved. The American state took advantage of its still dominant position to defend its own economic base, but this defensive posture could not provide a general solution to the problems facing all the developed capitalist economies, nor even create the basis for renewed US economic dynamism.[75] By the end of the seventies, with the American economy facing a flight of capital (both domestic and foreign), a Presidential report to Congress (describing itself as 'the most comprehensive and detailed analysis of the competitive position of the United States') confirmed a steep decline in competitiveness – one that it advised *could* be corrected, but not without a radical reorientation in economic policy to address the persistence of domestic inflation and the need for greater access to savings so as to accelerate investment.[76]

The concern with retaining capital and attracting new capital was especially crucial to what followed. The opening up of domestic and global capital markets was both an opportunity and a constraint for the American state. Liberalized finance held out the option of shifting an important aspect of competition to the very terrain on which the American economy potentially had its greatest advantages, yet those advantages could not become an effective instrument of American power until other economic and political changes had occurred. The American

49

state's ambivalence about how to deal with the growing strength of financial capital was reflected in its policies: capital controls were introduced in 1963, but were made open to significant 'exceptions'; the Euro-dollar market was a source of concern, but also recognized as making dollar holdings more attractive and subsequently encouraging the important recycling of petro-dollars to the third world. The liberalization of finance enormously strengthened Wall Street through the 1970s and, as Duménil and Lévy have persuasively shown, proved crucial to the broader changes that followed.[77] But this should not be seen as being at the expense of industrial capital. What was involved was not a 'financial coup', but rather a (somewhat belated) recognition on the part of American capital generally that the strengthening of finance was an essential, if sometimes painful, price to be paid for reconstituting American economic power.[78]

The critical 'turning point' in policy orientation came in 1979 with the 'Volcker shock' – the American state's self-imposed structural adjustment program. The Federal Reserve's determination to establish internal economic discipline by allowing interest rates to rise to historically unprecedented levels led to the vital restructuring of labour and industry and brought the confidence that the money markets and central bankers were looking for. Along with the more general neoliberal policies that evolved into a relatively coherent capitalist policy paradigm through the eighties, the new state-reinforced strength of finance set the stage for what came to be popularly known as 'globalization' – the accelerated drive to a seamless world of capital accumulation.

GLOBAL CAPITALISM AND AMERICAN EMPIRE

The mechanisms of neoliberalism (the expansion and deepening of markets and competitive pressures) may be economic, but neoliberalism was essentially a *political* response to the democratic gains that had been previously achieved by subordinate classes and which had become, in a new context and from capital's perspective, barriers to accumulation. Neoliberalism involved not just reversing those gains, but weakening their institutional foundations – including a shift in the hierarchy of state apparatuses in the US towards the Treasury and Federal Reserve at the expense of the old New Deal agencies. The US was of course not the only country to introduce neoliberal policies, but once the American state itself moved in this direction, it had a new status: capitalism now operated under 'a new form of social rule'[79] that promised, and largely delivered, (a) the revival of the productive base for American dominance; (b) a universal model for restoring the conditions for profits in other developed countries; and (c) the economic conditions for integrating global capitalism.

In the course of the economic restructuring that followed, American labour was further weakened, providing American capital with an even greater competitive flexibility vis-à-vis Europe. Inefficient firms were purged – a process that had been limited in the seventies. Existing firms restructured internally, outsourced processes to cheaper and more specialized suppliers, relocated to the increasingly urban southern states, and merged with other firms – all part of an accelerated reallocation of capital within the American economy. The new confidence of global investors (including Wall Street itself) in the

GLOBAL CAPITALISM AND AMERICAN EMPIRE

American economy and state provided the US with relatively cheap access to global savings and eventually made capital cheaper in the US. The available pools of venture capital enhanced investment in the development of new technologies (which also benefited from public subsidies via military procurement programs), and the new technologies were in turn integrated into management restructuring strategies and disseminated into sectors far beyond 'high tech'. The US proportion of world production did not further decline: it continued to account for around one-fourth of the total right into the twenty-first century.

The American economy not only reversed its slide in the 1980s, but also set the standards for European and Japanese capital to do the same.[80] The renewed confidence on the part of American capital consolidated capitalism as a global project through the development of new formal and informal mechanisms of international coordination. Neoliberalism reinforced the material and ideological conditions for guaranteeing 'national' treatment for foreign capital in each social formation, and for 'constitutionalizing' – by way of NAFTA, European Economic and Monetary Union and the WTO – the free flow of goods and capital (the WTO was a broader version of GATT, but with more teeth).[81]

The American economy's unique access to global savings through the central place of Wall Street within global money markets allowed it to import freely without compromising other objectives. This eventually brought to the American state the role, not necessarily intended, of 'importer of last resort' that limited the impact of slowdowns elsewhere, while also reinforcing foreign investors' and foreign exporters' dependence on American markets and state policies. The Federal Reserve, though allegedly concerned only with domestic policies, kept a steady eye on the international context. And the Treasury, whose relative standing within the state had varied throughout the post-war era, increasingly took on the role of global macro-economic manager through the 1980s and 1990s, thereby enhancing its status at the top of the hierarchy of US state apparatuses.[82]

The G-7 emerged as a forum for Ministers of Finance and Treasury officials to discuss global developments, forge consensus on issues and direction, and address in a concrete and controlled way any necessary exchange rate adjustments. The US allowed the Bank for International Settlements to re-emerge as major international coordinating agency, in the context of the greater role being played by increasingly 'independent' central bankers, to improve capital adequacy standards within banking systems. The IMF and the World Bank were also restructured. The IMF shifted from the 'adjustment' of balance of payments problems to addressing structural economic crises in third world countries (along the lines first imposed on Britain in 1976), and increasingly became the vehicle for imposing a type of conditionality, in exchange for loans, that incorporated global capital's concerns. The World Bank supported this, although by the 1990's, it also focused its attention on capitalist state-building – what it called 'effective states'.[83]

The reconstitution of the American empire in this remarkably successful fashion through the last decades of the twentieth century did not mean that global capitalism had reached a new plateau of stability. Indeed it may be said that dynamic instability and contingency are systematically incorporated into the reconstituted form of empire, in good part because the intensified competition characteristic of neoliberalism and the hyper-mobility of financial liberalization aggravate the uneven development and extreme volatility inherent in the global order. Moreover, this instability is dramatically amplified by the fact that the American state can only rule this order through other states, and turning them all into 'effective' states for global capitalism is no easy matter. It is the attempt by the American state to address these problems, especially vis-à-vis what it calls 'rogue states' in the third world, that leads American imperialism today to present itself in an increasingly unconcealed manner.

Beyond Inter-Imperial Rivalry

We cannot understand imperialism today in terms of the unresolved crisis of the 1970s, with overaccumulation and excess competition giving rise again to inter-imperial rivalry. The differences begin with the fact that while the earlier period was characterized by the relative economic strength of Europe and Japan, the current moment underlines their relative *weakness*. Concern with the American trade deficit seems to overlap both periods, but the context and content of that concern has radically changed. Earlier, the American deficit was just emerging, was generally seen as unsustainable even in the short run, and was characterized by foreign central bankers as exporting American inflation abroad. Today, the global economy has not only come to live with American trade deficits for a period approaching a quarter of a century, but global stability has come to depend on these deficits and it is the passage to their 'correction' that is the threat – this time a deflationary threat.

In the earlier period, global financial markets were just emerging; the issue this raised at the time was their impact

55

in undermining existing forms of national and international macro-management, including the international role of the American dollar. The consequent explosive development of financial markets has resulted in financial structures and flows that have now, however, made 'finance' itself a focal point of global macro-management – whether it be enforcing the discipline of accumulation, reallocating capital across sectors and regions, providing the investor/consumer credit to sustain even the modest levels of growth that have occurred, or supporting the capacity of the US economy to attract the global savings essential to reproducing the American empire.

In this context, the extent of the theoretically unself-conscious use of the term 'rivalry' to label the economic competition between the EU, Japan (or East Asia more broadly) and the United States is remarkable. The distinctive meaning the concept had in the pre-World War I context, when economic competition among European states was indeed imbricated with comparable military capacities and Lenin could assert that 'imperialist wars are absolutely inevitable',[84] is clearly lacking in the contemporary context of overwhelming American military dominance. But beyond this, the meaning it had in the past is contradicted by the distinctive economic as well as military integration that exists between the leading capitalist powers today.

The term 'rivalry' inflates economic competition between states far beyond what it signifies in the real world. While the conception of a transnational capitalist class, loosened from any state moorings or about to spawn a

GLOBAL CAPITALISM AND AMERICAN EMPIRE

supranational global state, is clearly exceedingly extravagant,[85] so too is any conception of a return to rival national bourgeoisies. The asymmetric power relationships that emerged out of the penetration and integration among the leading capitalist countries under the aegis of informal American empire were not dissolved in the wake of the crisis of the Golden Age and the greater trade competitiveness and capital mobility that accompanied it; rather they were refashioned and reconstituted through the era of neoliberal globalization.

None of this means, of course, that state and economic structures have become homogeneous or that there is no divergence in many policy areas, or that contradiction and conflict are absent from the imperial order. But these contradictions and conflicts are located not so much in the relationships between the advanced capitalist states as *within* these states, as they try to manage their internal processes of accumulation, legitimation and class struggle. This is no less true of the American state as it tries to manage and cope with the complexities of neo-imperial globalization.

Nor does the evolution of the European Union make the theory of inter-imperial rivalry relevant for our time.[86] Encouraged at its origins by the American state, its recent development through economic and monetary union – up to and including the launching of the Euro and the European Central Bank – has never been opposed by American capital within Europe, or by the American state. What it has accomplished in terms of free trade and capital mobility within its own region has fitted, rather than challenged, the American-led 'new form of social rule' that

57

GLOBAL CAPITALISM AND AMERICAN EMPIRE

neoliberalism represents. And what it has accomplished in terms of the integration of European capital markets has not only involved the greater penetration of American investment banking and its principle of 'shareholder value' inside Europe, but has, as John Grahl has shown, been 'based on the deregulation and internationalization of the US financial system.'[87]

The halting steps towards an independent European military posture, entirely apart from the staggering economic cost this would involve (all the more so in the context of relatively slow growth), were quickly put in perspective by the war on the former Yugoslavia over Kosovo – supported by every European government – through which the US made it very clear that NATO would remain the ultimate policeman of Europe.[88] But this only drove home a point over which pragmatic European politicians had never entertained any illusions. Dependence on American military technology and intelligence would still be such that the US itself sees '[a]n EU force that serves as an effective, if unofficial, extension of NATO rather than a substitute [as] well worth the trouble.'[89] And on the European side, Joschka Fischer, Germany's Foreign Minister, has similarly acknowledged that '[t]he transatlantic relationship is indispensable. The power of the United States is a decisive factor for peace and stability in the world. I don't believe Europe will ever be strong enough to look after its security alone.'[90]

Indeed, it is likely the very appreciation of this reality within European elite circles that lies at the heart of their oft-expressed frustrations with the current American leadership's tendency to treat them explicitly as merely 'junior' partners. Though it has been argued that the end of the Cold War left Europe less dependent on the American military umbrella and therefore freer to pursue its own interests, this same development also left the US freer to ignore European sensitivities.

As for East Asia, where Japan's highly centralized state might be thought to give it the imperial potential that the relatively loosely-knit EU lacks, it has shown even less capacity for regional let alone global leadership independent of the US. Its ability to penetrate East Asia economically, moreover, has been and remains mediated by the American imperial relationship.[91] This was particularly rudely underlined by the actions of the American Treasury (especially through the direct intervention of Rubin and Summers) in the East Asian crisis of 1997-98, when it dictated a harsh conditionality right in Japan's back yard.[92] Those who interpreted Japan's trade penetration of American markets and its massive direct foreign investments in the US through the 1980s in terms of inter-imperial rivalry betrayed a misleadingly economistic perspective. Japan remains dependent on American markets and on the security of its investments within the US, and its central bank is anxious to buy dollars so as limit the fall of the dollar and its impact on the Yen.

China may perhaps emerge eventually as a pole of inter-imperial power, but it will obviously remain very far from reaching such a status for a good many decades. The fact that certain elements in the American state are concerned to ensure that its 'unipolar' power today is used to prevent the possible emergence of imperial rivals tomorrow can hardly be used as evidence that such rivals already exist.

During the 1990s, not only the literal deflation of the Japanese economy, but also the slow growth and high unemployment in Europe stood in stark contrast with the American boom. So much was this the case that if Donald Sassoon was right to say that 'how to achieve the European version of the American society was the real political issue of the 1950s',[93] so it once again seemed to be the case in the 1990s, at least in terms of emulation of US economic policies and shareholder values. Now, with end of that boom, and the growing US trade and fiscal deficit, new predictions of American decline and inter-imperial rivalry have become commonplace. But the question of the sustainability of the American empire cannot be answered with such short-term and economistic measures, any more than they could in the 1970s, when Poulantzas properly disdained

> the various futurological analyses of the relative 'strength' or 'weakness' of the American and European economies, analyses which pose the question of inter-imperialist contradictions in terms of the 'competitiveness' and actual 'competition' between 'national economies'. In general, these arguments are restricted to 'economic criteria' which, considered in themselves, do not mean very much, …and [yet such analyses] extrapolate from these in quite an arbitrary manner.[94]

GLOBAL CAPITALISM AND AMERICAN EMPIRE

This is not to say that the current economic conjuncture does not reveal genuine economic problems for every state in global capitalism, including the American. These problems reflect not the continuation of the crisis of the 1970s, but rather new contradictions that the dynamic global capitalism ushered in by neoliberalism has itself generated, including the synchronization of recessions, the threat of deflation, the dependence of the world on American markets and the dependence of the United States on capital inflows to cover its trade deficit. There is indeed a systemic complexity in today's global capitalism that includes, even at its core, instabilities and even crises. Yet this needs to be seen not so much in terms of the old structural crisis tendencies and their outcomes, but as quotidian dimensions of contemporary capitalism's functioning and, indeed, as we argued above, even of its successes.

The issue for capitalist states is not preventing episodic crises – they will inevitably occur – but containing them. The American imperial state has, to date, demonstrated a remarkable ability to limit the duration, depth, and contagion of crises. And there is as yet little reason to expect that even the pressure on the value of the dollar today has become unmanageable. This is what lies behind the confidence of Andrew Crockett, general manager of the Bank for International Settlements and chairman of the Financial Stability Forum (comprising central bankers, finance ministry officials and market regulators from the G7 states) that 'they have the network of contacts, [and] the contingency plans, to deal with shocks to the markets.'[95] Of course such confidence does not itself guarantee that the US

Treasury and Federal Reserve, which worked closely with their counterparts in the other core capitalist states during the war on Iraq (whatever their governments' disagreements over that war) just as they did immediately after the disruption of Wall Street caused by the terrorist attacks of September 11,[96] will always have the capacity to cope with all contingencies. We would, however, argue that the future development of such capacities is not ruled out by any inherent *economic* contradictions alone.

The crisis that has produced an unconcealed American empire today lies, then, not in overaccumulation leading back to anything like inter-imperial rivalry, but in the limits that an informal empire based on ruling through other states sets for a strategy of coordinated economic growth, even among the advanced capitalist countries. In these liberal democratic states, the strength of domestic social forces – in spite of, and sometimes because of, the internationalization of domestic capital and the national state – has limited the adoption of neoliberalism (as seen, for example, in the difficulties experienced by the German state in introducing flexible labour markets, or the inertia of the Japanese state in restructuring its banking system). This has frustrated the 'reforms' that capital sees as necessary, along the lines of the American state's own earlier restructuring, to revive economic growth in these countries so as to allow them to share the burden of absorbing global imports and relieving pressure on the American trade deficit.

It is also by no means obvious, despite the energy that capitalists in each country have invested in securing these 'reforms', that they would, by themselves, prove to be the magic bullets that would produce renewed growth. And their full introduction could in any case generate far more intense class struggles from below – though it must be said that these would need to generate something approaching a fundamental transformation in class and state structures to generate a new alternative to neoliberalism and break the links with the American empire.

Unconcealed Empire: 'The Awesome Thing America is Becoming'

To the extent that there is a crisis of in imperialism today, it is best conceived as Poulantzas conceived the earlier crisis of the 1970s:

> What is currently in crisis is not directly American hegemony, under the impact of the 'economic power' of the other metropolises, whose rise would, according to some people have erected then automatically into equivalent 'counter-imperialisms', but rather imperialism as a whole, as a result of the world class struggles that have already reached the metropolitan zone itself. … In other words it is not the hegemony of American imperialism that is in crisis, but the whole of imperialism under this hegemony.[97]

The notion of 'world class struggles' is no doubt too loose, and in another sense too restrictive in light of the

64

GLOBAL CAPITALISM AND AMERICAN EMPIRE

diverse social forces now at play, to capture how the contradictions between the third world and the American empire are currently manifesting themselves. It is nevertheless the case that the most serious problems for 'imperialism as a whole' arise in relation to the states outside the capitalist core. Where these states are – as in much of the third world and the former Soviet bloc – relatively undeveloped capitalist states yet increasingly located within the orbit of global capital, the international financial institutions, as well as the core capitalist states acting either in concert or on their own, have intervened to impose 'economically correct' neoliberal structural 'reforms'. In the context of financial liberalization, this has meant a steady stream of economic crises. Some of these could be seen as a functionally necessary part of neoliberalism's success (as may perhaps be said of South Korea after the Asian crisis of 1997-8), but all too often these interventions have aggravated rather than solved the problem because of the abstract universalism of the remedy.

Whatever neoliberalism's successes in relation to strengthening an already developed capitalist economy, it increasingly appears as a misguided strategy for capitalist development itself. As for so-called 'rogue states' – those which are not within the orbit of global capitalism so that neither penetrating external economic forces nor international institutions can effectively restructure them – direct unilateral intervention on the part of the American state has become increasingly tempting. It is this that has brought the term 'empire' back into mainstream currency, and it is fraught with all kinds of unpredictable ramifications.

65

GLOBAL CAPITALISM AND AMERICAN EMPIRE

In this context, the collapse of the Communist world that stood outside the sphere of American empire and global capitalism for so much of the post-war era has become particularly important. On the one hand, the rapid penetration and integration by global capital and the institutions of informal American empire (such a NATO) of so much of what had been the Soviet bloc, and the opening of China, Vietnam, and even Cuba to foreign capital and their integration in world markets (even if under the aegis of Communist elites), has been remarkable. It has also removed the danger that direct US intervention in states outside the American hemisphere would lead to World War III and nuclear Armageddon.

The fact that even liberal human rights advocates and institutions through the 1990s have repeatedly called for the US to act as an international police power reflected the new conjuncture. But, on the other hand, both the hubris and sense of burden that came with the now evident unique power of the American state led it to question whether even the limited compromises it had to make in operating through multilateral institutions were unnecessarily constraining its strategic options, especially in relation to 'rogue states' outside the orbit of the informal empire.

The 'loneliness of power' was increasingly involved here. The felt burden of ultimate responsibility (and since 9/11 the much greater sensitivity to US vulnerability as a target of terrorism at home as well as abroad), promotes the desire to retain full 'sovereignty' to act as needed. This is what underlies the increasingly unconcealed nature of American imperialism. The problem it now faces in terms of 'conju-

66

GLOBAL CAPITALISM AND AMERICAN EMPIRE

gating its particular power with the general task of coordination' (to recall Anderson's incisive phrase), can clearly be seen not only in relation to the economic contradictions of neoliberalism discussed above, but also in the growing contradictions between nature and capitalism (as revealed, for example, not only in the severe problems of carbon emissions that the Kyoto Accord is supposed to address, but also in the problem of oil reserves addressed by the Cheney Report, discussed by Michael Klare in another essay in this volume).

These issues are multiplied all the more by the role the American imperial state now has come to play (and often to be expected to play) in maintaining social order around the whole globe. From the perspective of creating a 'world environment in which the American system can survive and flourish', the understanding of the 1950 National Security Council document NSC-68 that '[e]ven if there were no Soviet Union we would face the great problem... [that] the absence of order among nations is becoming less and less tolerable' anticipated what has finally become fully clear to those who run the American empire. George W. Bush's own National Security Strategy document of September 2002 (intimations of which were surfacing inside the American state as soon as the Soviet bloc collapsed)[98] had a long pedigree.

In this context, just as neoliberalism at home did not mean a smaller or weaker state, but rather one in which coercive apparatuses flourished (as welfare offices emptied out, the prisons filled up), so has neoliberalism led to the enhancement of the coercive apparatus the imperial state

67

GLOBAL CAPITALISM AND AMERICAN EMPIRE

needs to police social order around the world. The transformation of the American military and security apparatus through the 1990s in such a way as to facilitate this (analyzed by Paul Rogers elsewhere in this volume) can only be understood in this light. (US unilateralism in the use of this apparatus internationally is hardly surprising if we consider how the activities of the coercive apparatuses of states at a domestic level are protected from extensive scrutiny from legislatures, and from having to negotiate what they do with non-coercive state apparatuses.)

All this was already apparent in the responses to 'rogue states' under the Bush I and Clinton administrations. The US did work hard to win the UN's support for the 1990-91 Gulf War and oversaw the long regime of sanctions against Iraq that the American state insisted on through the 1990s. But other governments sensed a growing unilateralism on the part of the U.S. that made them increasingly nervous, if only in terms of maintaining their own states' legitimacy. The Gulf War had shown that the United Nations could be made to serve 'as an imprimatur for a policy that the United States wanted to follow and either persuaded or coerced everybody else to support,' as the Canadian ambassador to the UN put it at the time. This playing 'fast and loose with the provisions of the UN Charter' unnerved 'a lot of developing countries, which were privately outraged by what was going on but felt utterly impotent to do anything – a demonstration of the enormous US power and influence when it is unleashed.'[99]

Yet at the very same time, it also made American strategists aware just how little they could rely on the UN if they

68

had to go to such trouble to get their way. The United Nations, by its very nature as a quasi-parliamentary and diplomatic body made up of all the world's states, could not be as easily restructured as were the Bretton Woods institutions after the crisis of the 1970s. This, as evidenced in the repeated use of the American veto in the Security Council since that time, was a constant irritant. And while NATO could be relied on as a far more reliable vehicle for the American war on the former Yugoslavia over Kosovo (with the added benefit of making clear to the Europeans exactly who would continue to wield the international police power in their own backyard), even here the effort entailed in having to keep each and every NATO member onside was visibly resented within the American state itself.

Bush's isolationist rhetoric in the 2000 election campaign, questioning the need for American troops to get involved in remote corners of the globe, was bound to be reformulated once Bush was actually burdened with (and appropriately socialized in) the office of a Presidency that is now as inevitably imperial as is it domestic in nature. For this, the explicitly imperial statecraft that the geopolitical strategists close to the Republican Party had already fashioned was ready and waiting. September 11 alone did not determine their ascendancy in the state, but it certainly enhanced their status.

Their response has revealed all the tensions in the American state's combination of its imperial function of general coordination with the use of its power to protect and advance its national interests. Defining the security interests of global capitalism in a way that also serves the

69

needs of the American social formation and state becomes especially tricky once the security interests involved are so manifestly revealed as primarily American. This means that while threats to the US are still seen by it as an attack on global capitalism in general, the American state is increasingly impatient with making any compromises that get in the way of its acting on its own specific definition of the global capitalist interest and the untrammelled use of its particular state power to cope with such threats.

Perhaps the most important change in the administrative structure of the American empire in the transition from the Clinton administration to the Bush II administration has been the displacement of the Treasury from its pinnacle at the top of the state apparatus. The branches of the American state that control and dispense the means of violence are now in the driver's seat; in an Administration representing a Republican Party that has always been made up of a coalition of free marketeers, social conservatives and military hawks, the balance has been tilted decisively by September 11[100] towards the latter. But the unconcealed imperial face that the American state is now prepared to show to the world above all pertains to the increasing difficulties of managing a truly global informal empire – a problem that goes well beyond any change from administration to administration.

This could turn out to be a challenge as great as that earlier faced by formal empires with their colonial state apparatuses. The need to try to refashion all the states of the world so that they become at least minimally adequate for the administration of global order – and this is now also

GLOBAL CAPITALISM AND AMERICAN EMPIRE

seen as a general condition of the reproduction and extension of global capitalism – is now the central problem for the American state. But the immense difficulty of constructing outside the core anything like the dense networks that the new American imperialism succeeded in forging with the other leading capitalist states is clear from the only halting progress that has been made in extending the G7 even to the G8, let alone the G20. For the geopolitical stratum of the American state, this shows the limits of any 'effective states' approach outside the core based on economic linkages alone.

This explains not only the extension of US bases and the closer integration of intelligence and police apparatuses of all the states in the empire in the wake of September 11, but the harkening back to the founding moment of the post-1945 American empire in the military occupations of Japan and Germany as providing the model for restructuring Iraq within the framework of American empire. The logic of this posture points well beyond Iraq to all states 'disconnected from globalization', as a U.S. Naval War College professor advising the Secretary of Defense so chillingly put it:

> Show me where globalization is thick with
> network connectivity, financial transactions, liberal
> media flows, and collective security, and I will
> show you regions featuring stable governments,
> rising standards of living, and more deaths by
> suicide than murder. These parts of the world I call
> the Functioning Core... But show me where
> globalization is thinning or just plain absent, and I

71

GLOBAL CAPITALISM AND AMERICAN EMPIRE

will show you regions plagued by politically repressive regimes, widespread poverty and disease, routine mass murder, and – most important – the chronic conflicts that incubate the next generation of global terrorists. These parts of the world I call the non-integrating Gap... The real reason I support a war like this is that the resulting long-term military commitment will finally force America to deal with the entire Gap as a strategic threat environment.[101]

In this 'Gap' are listed Haiti, Colombia, Brazil and Argentina, Former Yugoslavia, Congo and Rwanda/Burundi, Angola, South Africa, Israel-Palestine, Saudi Arabia, Iraq, Somalia, Iran, Afghanistan, Pakistan, North Korea and Indonesia – to which China, Russia and India are added, for good measure, 'as new/integrating members of the core [that] may be lost in coming years.' The trouble for the American empire as it inclines in this strategic direction is that very few of the world's 'non-core' states today, given their economic and political structures and the social forces, are going to be able to be reconstructed along the lines of post-war Japan and Germany, even if (indeed especially if) they are occupied by the US military, and even if they are penetrated rather than marginalized by globalization. What is more, an American imperialism that is so blatantly imperialistic risks losing the very appearance of not being imperialist – that appearance which historically made it plausible and attractive.

The open disagreements over the war on Iraq between

GLOBAL CAPITALISM AND AMERICAN EMPIRE

the governments of France, Germany and even Canada, on the one hand, and the Bush administration, on the other, need to be seen in this light. These tensions pertain very little to economic 'rivalries'. The tensions pertain rather more to a preference on the part of these states themselves (in good part reflective of their relative lack of autonomous military capacity) for the use of international financial institutions, the WTO and the UN to try to fashion the 'effective states' around the world that global capitalism needs.

But the bourgeoisies of the other capitalist states are even less inclined to challenge American hegemony than they were in the 1970s. Indeed many capitalists in the other states inside the empire were visibly troubled by – and increasingly complained about – their states not singing from the same page as the Americans. In any case, the capitalist classes of each country, including the US (where many of the leading lights of financial capital, such as Rubin and Volcker, were openly disturbed by the posture of the Bush administration on the war as well as economic policy), were incapable of expressing a unified position either for or against the war. Once again we can see that what is at play in the current conjuncture is not contradictions between national bourgeoisies, but the contradictions of 'the whole of imperialism', implicating all the bourgeoisies that function under the American imperial umbrella.

These contradictions pertain most of all to the danger posed to the broader legitimacy of the other capitalist states now that they are located in a framework of American imperialism that is so unconcealed. The American empire

73

has certainly been hegemonic vis-à-vis these states, their capitalist classes and their various elite establishments, but it has never entailed, for all of the American economic and cultural penetration of their societies, a transfer of direct popular loyalty to the American state itself. Indeed, the American form of rule – founded on the constitutional principle of 'extensive empire and self-government' – has never demanded this. The economic and cultural emulation of the American way of life by so many ordinary people abroad may perhaps properly be spoken of as hegemony in Gramsci's terms. But however close the relationship between the American state and capitalist classes and their counterparts in the informal empire, this did not extend to anything like a sense of patriotic attachment to the American state among the citizenry of the other states.

Nor did the American state ever take responsibility for the incorporation, in the Gramscian sense of hegemony, of the needs of the subordinate classes of other states within its own construction of informal imperial rule. Their active consent to its informal imperial rule was always mediated by the legitimacy that each state could retain for itself and muster on behalf of any particular American state project – and this has often been difficult to achieve in the case of American coercive interventions around the globe over the past fifty years. A good many of these states thus distanced themselves from the repeated US interventions in Latin America and the Caribbean since 1945, and indeed since 1975, not to mention the American subversion of governments elsewhere, or the Vietnam War.

In this sense the unpopularity of American military

GLOBAL CAPITALISM AND AMERICAN EMPIRE

intervention – and even its lack of endorsement by other advanced capitalist states – is not new. But this dimension of the imperial order is proving to have particularly important consequences in the current conjuncture. The American state's war of aggression in Iraq – so flagrantly imperial and so openly connected to a doctrine that expresses the broader aim of securing a neoliberal capitalist order on a global scale – has evoked an unprecedented opposition, including within the capitalist core states. Yet even in France and Germany where the opposition is highest, many more people today attribute 'the problem with the US' as due to 'mostly Bush' rather than to the 'US in general'. This suggests that the possibility of a 'benign imperium' is still seen to exist even in the other advanced capitalist countries.[102] But insofar as the conditions making for American military intervention clearly transcend a given administration, and insofar as a benign imperium can hardly prove to be more than an illusion in today's world, this is a currency that could be less stable than the American dollar.

This is especially significant: since the American empire can only rule through other states, the greatest danger to it is that the states within its orbit will be rendered illegitimate by virtue of their articulation to the imperium. To be sure, only a fundamental change in the domestic balance of social forces and the transformation of the nature and role of those states can bring about their disarticulation from the empire, but the ideological space may now be opening up for the kind of mobilization from below, combining the domestic concerns of subordinate classes and other

GLOBAL CAPITALISM AND AMERICAN EMPIRE

oppressed social forces with the anti-globalization and anti-war movements, that can eventually lead to this.

It is the fear of this that fuels, on the one hand, the pleas of those who entreat the imperium to be more benign and to present itself in a more multilateralist fashion, at least symbolically; and, on the other hand, the actions of those who are using the fear of terrorism to close the space for public dissent within each state. This is especially so within the United States itself. The old question posed by those who, at the founding of the American state, questioned whether an extended empire could be consistent with republican liberty – posed again and again over the subsequent two centuries by those at home who stood up against American imperialism – is back on the agenda. The need to sustain intervention abroad by mobilizing support and limiting opposition through instilling fear and repression at home raises the prospect that the American state may become more authoritarian internally as part of it becoming more blatantly aggressive externally. But the unattractiveness of an empire that is no longer concealed in its coercive nature at home as well as abroad suggests that anti-imperialist struggles – even in the rich capitalist states at the heart of the empire as well as in the poor ones at its extremities – will have growing mass appeal and force.

NOTES

1 'Great Britain, The United States and Canada', Twenty-First Cust Foundation Lecture, University of Nottingham, May 21, 1948, in H. Innis, *Essays in Canadian Economic History*, Toronto: University of Toronto Press, 1956, p. 407.

2 The Friedman manifesto appeared in the *New York Times Magazine* on March 28, 1999, and the Ignatieff essay on January 5, 2003. Ignatieff adds: 'It means laying down the rules America wants (on everything from markets to weapons of mass destruction) while exempting itself from other rules (the Kyoto protocol on climate change and the International Criminal Court) that go against its interests.'

3 *The Grand Chessboard*, New York: Basic Books, 1997, p. 40.

4 See 'Rebuilding America's Defenses: Strategy, Forces and Resources For a New Century', A Report of the Project for the New American Century. http://www.newamericancentury.org/publicationsreports.htm; and *The National Security Strategy of the United States of America*, Falls Village, Connecticut: Winterhouse, 2002.

5 Antonio Santosuosso, *Storming the Heavens: Soldiers, Emperor, and Civilians in the Roman Empire*, Westview: Boulder, 2001, pp. 151-2.

6 *Monthly Review* 42(6), 1990, pp. 1-6. For two of those who insisted, from different perspectives, on the need to retain the concept of imperialism, see Susan Strange, 'Towards a Theory of Transnational Empire', in E-O. Czempiel and J. Rosenau, eds., *Global Changes and Theoretical Challenges*, Lexington: Lexington Books, 1989, and Peter Gowan, 'Neo-Liberal Theory and Practice for Eastern Europe', *New Left Review*, 213, 1995.

7 Gareth Stedman Jones, 'The Specificity of US Imperialism' *New Left Review*, 60 (first series), 1970, p. 60, n. 1.

8 Giovanni Arrighi, *The Geometry of Imperialism*, London: NLB, 1978, p. 17. What in good part lay behind the left's disenchantment with the concept of imperialism was the extent to which the words that opened Kautsky's infamous essay in 1914 – the one that so attracted

GLOBAL CAPITALISM AND AMERICAN EMPIRE

Lenin's ire – increasingly rang true: 'First of all, we need to be clear what we understand from the term imperialism. This word is used in every which way, but the more we discuss and speak about it the more communication and understanding becomes weakened.' 'Der Imperialismus', *Die Neue Ziet*, Year 32, XXXII/2, Sept 11th, 1914, p. 908. Only the last part of this famous essay was translated and published in *New Left Review* in 1970. Thanks are due to Sabine Neidhardt for providing us with a full translation. Note Arrighi's use of almost identical words in 1990: 'What happened to the term imperialism is by the time it flourished in the early 1970s, it had come to mean everything and therefore nothing.' See 'Hegemony and Social Change', *Mersham International Studies Review*, 38, 1994, p. 365.

9   Bob Rowthorn, 'Imperialism in the Seventies: Unity or Rivalry', *New Left Review*, 69, 1971.

10   'In recent years no topic has occupied the attention of scholars of international relations more than that of American hegemonic decline. The erosion of American economic political and military power is unmistakable. The historically unprecedented resources and capabilities that stood behind United States early postwar diplomacy, and that led Henry Luce in the 1940s to herald an "American century," have given way to an equally remarkable and rapid redistribution of international power and wealth. In the guise of theories of "hegemonic stability," scholars have been debating the extent of hegemonic decline and its consequences.' G. John Ikenberry, 'Rethinking the Origins of American Hegemony', *Political Science Quarterly*, 104(3), 1989, p. 375. Among the few critics of this view, see Bruce Russett, 'The Mysterious Case of Vanishing Hegemony. Or is Mark Twain Really Dead?', *International Organization*, 39(2), 1985; Stephen Gill, 'American Hegemony: Its Limits and Prospects in the Reagan Era', *Millenium*, 15(3), 1986; and Susan Strange, 'The Persistent Myth of Lost Hegemony', *International Organization*, 41(4), 1987.

11   Andrew Glyn and Bob Sutcliffe, 'Global But Leaderless', *Socialist*

12 Bruce Cumings. 'Global Realm with no Limit, Global Realm with no Name', *Radical History Review*, 57, 1993, pp. 47-8. This issue of the journal was devoted to a debate on 'Imperialism: A Useful Category of Analysis?'.

13 Andrew L. Bacevich, *American Empire: The Realities and Consequences of U.S. Diplomacy,* Cambridge, MA: Harvard University Press, 2002, pp. x, 3, 219.

14 Michael Hardt and Antonio Negri, *Empire*, Cambridge, MA: Harvard University Press, 2000, p. xiv, emphasis in text. See our review essay, 'Gems and Baubles in Empire', *Historical Materialism*, 10, 2002, pp. 17-43.

15 *The Great Transformation*, Beacon, Boston: 1957, p. 18.

16 Philip McMichael, 'Revisiting the Question of the Transnational State: A Comment on William Robinson's "Social theory and Globalization"', *Theory and Society*, 30, 2001, p. 202.

17 Just how far this fundamental mistake continues to plague the Left can be discerned from the fact that even those who insist today that the old theory of imperialism no longer can be made to fit contemporary global capitalism, nevertheless accept it as explaining the pre-World War One imperialism. This has been most recently seen in the way Hardt and Negri completely follow Lenin and Luxemburg in this respect, arguing that capitalism by its very nature confronts a contradiction in trying to realize surplus value: workers get less than what they produce (underconsume), so capital must look outside its own borders for markets. Since this is a problem in each capitalist country, the 'solution' requires constant access to markets in *non-capitalist* social formations. The focus on non-capitalist markets is reinforced by the need for the raw materials to feed workers and supply production at home. But the successful realization of the surplus and the expansion of production simply recreate the contradiction or crisis of underconsumption as a crisis of overproduction. This forces capital 'abroad' to find outlets for its surplus capital. That overall search for foreign markets, materials and invest-

79

GLOBAL CAPITALISM AND AMERICAN EMPIRE

ment opportunities involves the extension of national sovereignty beyond its borders – imperialism – and at the same time tends to bring the outside world 'in' (i.e. into capitalism). And so the crisis of underconsumption/overproduction is simply regenerated on a larger scale.

18 '[I]f capitalism could raise the living standards of the masses, who in spite of the amazing technical progress are everywhere still half-starved and poverty stricken, there could be no question of a surplus of capital.... But if capitalism did these things it would not be capitalism; for both the uneven development and a semi-starvation level of existence of the masses are fundamental and inevitable conditions and constitute premises of this mode of production.' V.I. Lenin, *Imperialism: The Highest Stage of Capitalism*, in *Selected Works*, Volume I, Moscow: Progress Publishers, 1970, p. 716.

19 *Ibid.*

20 See John Willoughby, *Capitalist Imperialism: Crisis and the State*, New York: Harwood Academic Publishers, 1986, esp. pp. 7-8; and earlier, put more circumspectly, Harry Magdoff, *The Age of Imperialism*, New York: Monthly Review Press, 1969, esp. p. 13.

21 See John Kautsky, 'J.A. Schumpeter and Karl Kautsky: Parallel Theories of Imperialism', *Midwest Journal of Political Science*, V(2), 1961, pp. 101-128; and Lenin, *Imperialism*, p. 715.

22 Ellen Meiksins Wood, *Empire of Capital*, London: Verso, 2003, p. 72.

23 John Gallagher and Ronald Robinson, 'The Imperialism of Free Trade', *The Economic History Review*, VI(1), 1953, p. 6. They explicitly challenged Lenin's view that the move towards responsible government in the colonies that coincided with the era of free trade did not mean that the policy of 'free competition' entailed 'that the liberation of the colonies and their complete separation from Great Britain was inevitable and desirable' in the opinion of leading bourgeois politicians. This reflected, they argued, a conventional misconception that free trade rendered empire 'superfluous', which severely misconstrued the significance of changes in constitutional forms. As Gallagher and Robinson put it: '[R]esponsible government

GLOBAL CAPITALISM AND AMERICAN EMPIRE

far from being a separatist device, was simply a change from direct to indirect methods of maintaining British interests. By slackening the formal political bond at the appropriate time, it was possible to rely on economic dependence and mutual good-feeling to keep the colonies bound to Britain while still using them as agents for further British expansion.' *Ibid.*, p. 2.

24 *Ibid.*, pp. 6-7.

25 All the quotations of Karl Kautsky here are from John Kautsky, 'J.A. Schumpeter and Karl Kautsky', pp. 114-116, except for the one on his economic reductionism, where we have used the wording of *New Left Review*'s 1970 partial translation of 'Der Imperialismus', p. 46. For the best exposition of Kautsky's conception of 'ultra-imperialism', see Massimo Salvadori, *Karl Kautsky and the Socialist Revolution, 1880-1933*, London: NLB, 1979, pp. 169-203.

26 These are the words of a biographer of Dean Acheson, as quoted by William Appleman Williams, *Empire as a Way of Life*, New York: Oxford University Press, 1980, p. 185.

27 Perry Anderson, 'Force and Consent', *New Left Review*, 17, 2002, p. 24.

28 *Ibid.*, p. 25. See also Daniel Lazare's *The Frozen Republic*, New York: Harcourt Brace, 1996 which fails to distinguish between the democratic constraints and domestic policy gridlocks that the old elitist system of checks and balances produces and the remarkable informal imperial 'carrying power' of the American constitution in the sense argued here.

29 Quoted in Williams, *Empire as a Way of Life*, p. 61. Jefferson had already come to accept Madison's 'expansionist' perspective that republican liberty was not incompatible with an extended state, nor with a strong federal government. As DeVoto sums up Jefferson's trajectory: '...after 1803, the phrase "the United States" in Jefferson's writings, usually plural up to now, begins increasingly to take a singular verb.' Bernard DeVoto, *The Course of Empire*, Lincoln: University of Nebraska Press, 1983 (1952), p. 403.

30 See Hardt and Negri, *Empire*, chapter 2.5.

GLOBAL CAPITALISM AND AMERICAN EMPIRE

31   See John F. Manley, 'The Significance of Class in American History and Politics', in L.C. Didd and C. Jilson, eds., *New Perspectives on American Politics*, Washington, D.C.: Congressional Quarterly Press, 1994, esp. pp. 16-19.

32   Quoted in Williams, *Empire as a Way of Life,* p. 43.

33   *The Federalist Papers*, No. 11 (Hamilton), Clinton Rossiter, ed., New York: Mentor, 1999, p. 59.

34   See Marc Engel, *A Mighty Empire: The Origins of the American Revolution*, Ithaca: Cornell University Press, 1988.

35   DeVoto, *The Course of Empire*, p. 275.

36   See Charles C. Bright, 'The State in the United States During the Nineteenth Century', in C. Bright and S. Harding, eds., *Statemaking and Social Movements*, Ann Arbor: University of Michigan Press, 1984.

37   See the first two chapters of Gabriel Kolko's *Main Currents in Modern American History*, New York: Harper & Row, 1976; and Bright, 'The State', esp. pp. 145-153.

38   Anderson, 'Force and Consent', p. 25.

39   S.S. Roberts, 'An Indicator of Informal Empire: Patterns of U.S. Navy Cruising on Overseas Stations, 1869-97', Center for Naval Analysis, Alexandria, Virginia, n.d., cited in Williams, p. 122.

40   Stedman Jones, 'The Specificity', p. 63.

41   See L. Panitch, 'Class and Dependency in Canadian Political Economy', *Studies in Political Economy*, 6, 1980, pp. 7-34; W. Clement, *Continental Corporate Power*, Toronto: McLelland & Stewart, 1977; and M. Wilkins, *The Emergence of Multinational Enterprise*, Cambridge, Mass: 1970. Jefferson had justified the war of 1812 (sparked by American concerns that the British were encouraging Indian resistance to western expansion) in these terms: 'If the British don't give us the satisfaction we demand, we will take Canada, which wants to enter the union; and when, together with Canada, we shall have the Floridas, we shall no longer have any difficulties with our neighbors; and it is the only way of preventing them.' The passage from the urge to continental expansion though internal empire to expansion

GLOBAL CAPITALISM AND AMERICAN EMPIRE

through informal external empire, with Canada representing the model of successful American imperialism in the twentieth century, was marked, almost exactly 100 years later, when President Taft spoke in terms of 'greater economic ties' being the way to make Canada 'only an adjunct of the USA.' See Williams, pp. 63-4, 132.

42 Quoted in G. Achcar, *The Clash of Barbarisms*, New York: Monthly Review Press, 2002, p. 96.

43 Letter to Duncan Grant, quoted in Nicholas Fraser, 'More Than Economist', *Harper's Magazine*, November, 2001, p. 80. The issue here, of course, was the American state's refusal to forgive Allied war debts, with all the consequences this entailed for the imposition of heavy German reparations payments. See Michael Hudson's *Super Imperialism: The Economic Strategy of American Empire*, New York: Holt, Rinehart and Winston, 1971.

44 See R. Jeffery Lustig, *Corporate Liberalism: The Origins of American Political Theory 1890-1920*, Berkeley: University of California Press, 1982; and Stephen Skowronek, *Building a New American State: The Expansion of National Administrative Capacities 1877-1920*, New York: Cambridge University Press, 1982.

45 See Kees van der Pijl, *The Making of an Atlantic Ruling Class*, London: Verso, 1984, p. 93.

46 This was glimpsed by Charles and Mary Beard even before the war in their analysis of the passage from the old 'Imperial Isolationism' to the newer 'Collective Internationalism' in their *America in Midpassage*, New York: Macmillan, 1939, Volume I, Ch. X, and Vol, II, Ch. XVII.

47 This and the subsequent quotations in this section are all from Brian Waddell, *The War against the New Deal: World War II and American Democracy*, De Kalb: Northern Illinois University Press: 2001, pp. 4-5. See also, Rhonda Levine, *Class Struggles and the New Deal*, Lawrence: University Press of Kansas, 1988.

48 Brian Waddell, 'Corporate Influence and World War II: Resolving the New Deal Political Stalemate', *Journal of Political History*, 11(3), 1999, p. 2.

GLOBAL CAPITALISM AND AMERICAN EMPIRE

49 Geir Lundestad, 'Empire by Invitation? The United States and Western Europe, 1945-52', *Journal of Peace Research,* 23(3), September, 1986; and see van der Pijl, *The Making,* chapter 6.

50 See Gabriel Kolko, *The Politics of War: The World and United States Foreign Policy 1943-1945,* New York: Random House, 1968.

51 See Eric Helleiner, *States and the Reemergence of Global Finance,* Ithaca: Cornell, 1994.

52 Robert Skidelsky, *John Maynard Keynes: Fighting for Freedom, 1937-1946,* New York: Viking, 2001, pp. xxiii.

53 *The United States in a New World: I. Relations with Britain. A series of reports on potential courses for democratic action. Prepared under the auspices of the Editors of Fortune,* May, 1942, pp. 9-10.

54 'An American Proposal', *Fortune,* May 1942, pp. 59-63.

55 All the quotations in this and the previous paragraph are derived from Skidelsky's account, pp. 334, 348, 350-1, 355.

56 The very words which senior officials at the German Bundesbank used in an interview we conducted in October, 2002.

57 Martin Shaw, *Theory of the Global State,* Cambridge, U.K.: Cambridge University Press, 2000.

58 Bacevich, *American Empire,* p. 4.

59 Peter Gowan, 'The American Campaign for Global Sovereignty', *Socialist Register 2003,* London: Merlin, 2003, p. 5.

60 Michael Barratt Brown, *The Economics of Imperialism,* Middlesex, UK: Penguin, 1974, pp. 208-9.

61 See Raymond Aron, *The Imperial Republic: The United States and the World 1945-1973,* Cambridge, MA: Winthrop, 1974, esp. pp. 168 and 217; and N. Poulantzas, *Classes in Contemporary Capitalism,* London: NLB, 1974, esp. pp. 39 and 57.

62 Alan S. Milward, *The European Rescue of the Nation-State,* London: Routledge, 2000.

63 See Robert Cox, *Production, Power and World Order,* New York: Columbia University Press, 1987, esp. p. 254. Cf. N. Poulantzas, *Classes,* p. 73.

64 Address on Foreign Economic Policy, Delivered at Baylor

GLOBAL CAPITALISM AND AMERICAN EMPIRE

University, March 6, 1947, Public Papers of the Presidents, http://www.trumanlibrary.org/trumanpapers/pppus/1947/52.htm. On the preparations for this crucial speech, see Gregory A. Fossendal, *Our Finest Hour: Will Clayton, the Marshall Plan, and the Triumph of Democracy*, Stanford: Hoover Press, 1993, pp. 213-5.

65   Quoted in Williams, p. 189; and see Gabriel Kolko, *Century of War*, New York: The New Press, 1994, p. 397.

66   The special post-war conditions included the application of technologies developed during the war; catch up to American technology and methods (the gap had already been rising during the thirties and obviously accelerated during the war); pent-up demand; subsidized investments for rebuilding and the productivity effect of new facilities – all providing enormous scope for accumulation after the destruction of so much value during the Depression and the War. See Moses Abramowitz, 'Catching Up, Forging Ahead, and Falling Behind', *Journal of Economic History*, 46(2), June, 1986, and also 'Rapid Growth Potential and Realization: The Experience of the Capitalist Economies in the Postwar Period' in Edmund Malinvaud, ed., *Economic Growth and Resources,* London: Macmillan, 1979. Also crucial was the unique role of the American state in opening up its market, providing critical financial assistance, and contributing to international economic and political stability internationally.

67   The interwar collapse of the gold standard had demonstrated that capital mobility and democratic pressures from below, which limited any 'automatic' adjustment process, were incompatible with stable exchange rates.

68   On the relationship between the collapse of the gold standard, capital mobility, and the development of democratic pressures, see Barry Eichengreen, *Globalizing Capital: A History of the International Monetary System*, Princeton: Princeton University Press, 1996, Chapters 2-3. On the developments within US finance itself in the 1970s, and their impact abroad, see Michael Moran, *The Politics of the Financial Services Revolution*, London: Macmillan, 1991.

69   Looking back to that period, two Vice-Presidents of Citibank,

GLOBAL CAPITALISM AND AMERICAN EMPIRE

observed 'it is not surprising that economists were so sure in the late 60's and early 70's that the breakdown of fixed exchange rates would further weaken economic links between countries.' See H. Cleveland and R. Bhagavatula, 'The Continuing World Economic Crisis', *Foreign Affairs,* 59(3), 1981, p. 600. See also Louis Pauly's observation that, at the time, '[i]nternational monetary disarray appeared quite capable of restoring the world of the 1930s'. Louis B. Pauly, *Who Elected the Bankers?*, Ithaca: Cornell University Press, 1997, p. 100.

70 The 'induced reproduction of American monopoly capitalism within the other metropolises…implies the extended reproduction within them of the political and ideological conditions for [the] development of American imperialism.' N. Poulantzas, 1974, p. 47.

71 'It is this dis-articulation and heterogeneity of the domestic bourgeoisie that explains the weak resistance, limited to fit and starts, that European states have put up to American capital'. *Ibid.*, p. 75.

72 *Ibid.*, p. 87.

73 *Ibid.*, p. 81. On the internationalization of the state, see also Cox, *Production, Power, And World Order*, pp. 253-267.

74 At one time or another, policy during the seventies included import surcharges, attempts at international co-operation on exchange rates, wage and price controls, monetarism, and fiscal stimulus.

75 A *New York Times* reporter captured the unilateralist aggressiveness driving the American response: 'What is entirely clear is that the United States in a single dramatic stroke has shown the world how powerful it still is… in breaking the link between the dollar and gold and imposing a 10% import tax, the United States has shown who is Gulliver and who the Lilliputians… by "Lilliputians" are meant not the Nicaraguans or Gabons but West Germany, Japan, Britain, and the other leading industrial nations', cited by H.L. Robinson, 'The Downfall of the Dollar' in *Socialist Register 1973*, London: Merlin Press, 1973, p. 417.

76 *Report of the President on U.S. Competitiveness*, Washington: Office of Foreign Economic Research, U.S. Department of Labour,

September, 1980.

77   G. Duménil and D. Lévy, 'The Contradictions of Neoliberalism' in *Socialist Register 2002*, London: Merlin, 2002.

78   Our interviews with key industrial and financial figures, including in September 2001 Richard Wagoner, CEO of General Motors, and in March 2003 Paul Volcker, the former Chairman of the Federal Reserve who also led the negotiations with Chrysler, have confirmed us in this view. In spite of the fact that the auto industry was hit especially hard by the high interest rates, high dollar, and reduction in consumer demand that came with the shift to financial liberalization, industry executives considered this direction as being the only alternative through the eighties and nineties.

79   The term is from G. Albo and T. Fast's 'Varieties of Neoliberalism' paper presented to the Conference on the Convergence of Capitalist Economies, Wake Forest, North Carolina September 27-29, 2002.

80   See S. Gindin and L. Panitch, 'Rethinking Crisis', *Monthly Review,* November, 2002.

81   See Stephen Gill, *Power and Resistance in the New World Order*, London: Palgrave-Macmillan, 2003, pp. 131ff. and pp. 174ff.

82   See Leo Panitch, 'The New Imperial State', *New Left Review*, 2, 2000.

83   See Leo Panitch, '"The State in a Changing World": Social-Democratizing Global Capitalism?', *Monthly Review,* October, 1998.

84   Lenin, preface to the French and German editions of *Imperialism,* p. 674.

85   Compare W. Ruigrok and R. van Tulder, *The Logic of International Restructuring*, London: Routledge, 1995 (esp. chs. 6 & 7) against W.I. Robinson, 'Beyond Nation-State Paradigms', *Sociological Forum*, 13(4), 1998; and see the debate on Robinson's 'Towards a Global Ruling Class?', *Science and Society*, 64(1), 2000 in the 'Symposium' in 65(4) of that journal, 2001-2.

86   The argument here is much further elaborated in L. Panitch and S. Gindin, 'Euro-capitalism and American Empire', *Studies in Political Economy*, Fall 2003.

GLOBAL CAPITALISM AND AMERICAN EMPIRE

87   John Grahl, 'Globalized Finance: The Challenge to the Euro', *New Left Review*, 8, 2001, p. 44. See also his outstanding paper, 'Notes on Financial Integration and European Society', presented to conference on The Emergence of a New Euro-Capitalism, Marburg, October 2002. On the increasing adoption of American management practices in Europe, see M. Carpenter and S. Jefferys, *Management, Work and Welfare in Western Europe*, London: Edward Elgar, 2000.

88   See Peter Gowan, 'Making Sense of NATO's War on Yugoslavia', *Socialist Register 2000*, London: Merlin, 2000.

89   W.A. Hay and H. Sicherman, 'Europe's Rapid Reaction Force: What, Why, And How?', *Foreign Policy Research Institute*, February, 2001.

90   *Economist,* May 27, 2003.

91   See Dan Bousfield, 'Export-Led Development and Imperialism: A Response to Burkett and Hart-Landsberg', *Historical Materialism*, 11(1), 2003, pp. 147-160. The counter argument, in terms of Japan's 'leadership from behind' was best set out in G. Arrighi and B. Silver, ed., *Chaos and Governance in the World System*, Minneapolis: University of Minnesota Press, 1999.

92   See Panitch, 'The New Imperial State'.

93   Donald Sassoon, *One Hundred Years of Socialism*, London: I.B. Taurus, 1996, p. 207.

94   Poulantzas, *Classes*, pp. 86-7.

95   *Financial Times*, March 26, 2003.

96   Our interviews at the Bundesbank and the UK Treasury in October 2002 confirm this. Indeed, there often appears to be more contact across the Atlantic between these bureaucrats and their counterparts in the US than there is among the various departments within these institutions.

97   *Classes in Contemporary Capitalism*, p. 87.

98   See Peter Gowan, 'The American Campaign', pp. 8-10.

99   'The United Nations after the Gulf War: A Promise Betrayed', Stephen Lewis interviewed by Jim Wurst, *World Policy Journal*,

GLOBAL CAPITALISM AND AMERICAN EMPIRE

Summer 1991, pp. 539-49.

100   The increased influence gained by the military, coercive and security apparatuses in the wake of September 11 could be seen in that the first victory of the new war was scored at home, against the US Treasury. It involved breaking the latter's long-standing resistance (lest it would demonstrate the continuing viability of capital controls) to freezing bank accounts allegedly connected to terrorist organizations (which mechanisms the US state has always known about since it was involved in establishing these to facilitate money transfers to many of its favoured terrorists in the past).

101   Thomas P.M. Barnett, 'The Pentagon's New Map: It Explains Why We're Going to War and Why We'll Keep Going to War', *Esquire*, March, 2003 (available at the U.S. Naval War College website at http://www.nwc.navy.mil/newrules/ThePentagonsNewMap.htm).

102   See the report on the Pew Global Attitudes Survey in the *Financial Times*, June 4, 2003, which shows that in France and Germany, where only 43% and 45% respectively have 'a favourable image of the US' today, 74% of respondents in each country attribute the problem with the US to 'mostly Bush' as opposed to only 25% to the 'US in general' or to 'both'. Interestingly, in those advanced capitalist countries where the US image is more positive (Canada 63%, the UK 70%) there is nevertheless a higher percentage than in France or Germany who see 'the problem with the US' as due to the 'US in general' or 'both' (32%) rather than 'mostly Bush' (60%). As for countries like Indonesia and Turkey, where 'a favourable image of the US' has fallen from 75% and 53% respectively to only 15% today in both countries, it may be worth noting that whereas 45% of Turks attribute the problem to the 'US in general' or 'both', only 27% of Indonesians do so, in contrast with the 69% who see the problem as 'mostly Bush'.

89

Socialist Register – Published Annually Since 1964

Leo Panitch and Colin Leys – Editors
2004: THE NEW IMPERIAL CHALLENGE

How should we face the new imperial challenge presented by the US today? How should we understand imperialism and its relationship to globalized capitalism?

Contents: Leo Panitch & Sam Gindin: Global Capitalism and American Empire; Aijaz Ahmad: Imperialism of Our Time; David Harvey: The 'New' Imperialism – Accumulation by Dispossession; Gregory Albo: The Old and New Economics of Imperialism; Noam Chomsky: Truths and Myths About the Invasion of Iraq; Amy Bartholomew & Jennifer Breakspear: Human Rights as Swords of Empire; Paul Rogers: The US Military Posture – 'A Uniquely Benign Imperialism'?; Michael T. Klare: Blood for Oil – The Bush-Cheney Energy Strategy; John Bellamy Foster & Brett Clark: Ecological Imperialism – The Curse of Capitalism; Tina Wallace: NGO Dilemmas – Trojan Horses for Global Neoliberalism?; John S. Saul: Globalization, Imperialism, Development – False Binaries and Radical Resolutions; Emad El-Din Aysha: The Limits and Contradictions of 'Americanization'; Bob Sutcliffe: Crossing Borders in the New Imperialism.

290 pp. 234 x 156 mm.

0850365341 hardback 085036535X paperback

Canada: Fernwood Publishing; USA: Monthly Review Press; UK and Rest of World: Merlin Press

Leo Panitch and Colin Leys – Editors
2003: FIGHTING IDENTITIES – Race, Religion and Ethno-Nationalism

"these contributions ... show a left able to avoid both economic reductionism and post-modern identity-fetishism in confronting and understanding a world of mounting anxiety, instability and violence." Stephen Marks, *Tribune*.

Contents: Peter Gowan: The American Campaign for Global Sovereignty; Aziz Al-Azmeh: Postmodern Obscurantism and 'the Muslim Question'; Avishai Ehrlich: Palestine, Global Politics and Israeli Judaism; Susan Woodward: The Political Economy of Ethno-Nationalism in Yugoslavia; Georgi Derluguian: How Soviet Bureaucracy Produced Nationalism and what came of it in Azerbaijan; Pratyush Chandra: Linguistic-Communal Politics and Class Conflict in India; Mahmood Mamdani: Making Sense of Political Violence in Postcolonial Africa; Hugh Roberts: The Algerian Catastrophe: Lessons for the Left; Stephen Castles: The International Politics of Forced Migration; Hans-Georg Betz: Xenophobia, Identity Politics and Exclusionary Populism in Western Europe; Jörg Flecker: The European Right and Working Life- From ordinary miseries to political disasters; Huw Beynon & Lou Kushnick: Cool Britannia or Cruel Britannia? Racism and New Labour; Bill Fletcher Jr. & Fernando Gapasin: The Politics of Labour and Race in the USA; Amory Starr: Is the North American Anti-Globalization Movement Racist? Critical reflections; Stephanie Ross: Is This What Democracy Looks Like? -The politics of the anti-globalization movement in North America; Sergio Baierle: The Porto Alegre Thermidor: Brazil's 'Participatory Budget' at the crossroads; Nancy Leys Stepan: Science and Race: Before and after the Genome Project; John S. Saul: Identifying Class, Classifying Difference.

396pp, 234x156mm

0850365074 hardback 0850365082 paperback

Canada: Fernwood Publishing; USA: Monthly Review Press; UK and Rest of World: Merlin Press

Leo Panitch and Colin Leys – Editors
2002: A WORLD OF CONTRADICTIONS

Timely and critical analysis of what big businesses and their governments want, and of the problems they create.

Contents: Naomi Klein: Farewell To 'The End Of History':Organization And Vision In Anti-Corporate Movements; André Drainville: Québec City 2001 and The Making Of Transnational Subjects; Gérard Duménil & Dominique Lévy: The Nature and Contradictions of Neoliberalism; Elmar Altvater: The Growth Obsession; David Harvey The Art Of Rent: Globalization, Monopoly and The Commodification of Culture; Graham Murdock & Peter Golding: Digital Possibilities, Market Realities: The Contradictions of Communications Convergence; Reg Whitaker: The Dark Side of Life: Globalization and International Crime; Guglielmo Carchedi: Imperialism, Dollarization and The Euro; Susanne Soederberg: The New International Financial Architecture: Imposed Leadership and 'Emerging Markets'; Paul Cammack: Making Poverty Work; Marta Russell & Ravi Malhotra: Capitalism and Disability; Michael Kidron: The Injured Self; David Miller: Media Power and Class Power: Overplaying Ideology; Pablo Gonzalez Casanova: Negotiated Contradictions; Ellen Wood: Contradictions: Only in Capitalism?

293pp, 234 x156mm

0850365023 hardback 085036501 5 paperback

Canada: Fernwood Publishing; USA: Monthly Review Press; UK and Rest of World: Merlin Press

---

For information on previous editions of the Socialist Register and other books from the Merlin Press visit our web site: www.merlinpress.co.uk